Quincy Blakeley

A Historical Discourse delivered at the Centennial

Celebration of the Congregational Church in Campton

Quincy Blakeley

A Historical Discourse delivered at the Centennial Celebration of the Congregational Church in Campton

ISBN/EAN: 9783337236281

Printed in Europe, USA, Canada, Australia, Japan

Cover: Foto ©Lupo / pixelio.de

More available books at **www.hansebooks.com**

A

HISTORICAL DISCOURSE

DELIVERED AT THE

CENTENNIAL CELEBRATION

OF THE

Congregational Church in Campton, N.H.

OCTOBER 20, 1874,

By Rev. QUINCY BLAKELY,

PASTOR OF THE CHURCH,

AND

OTHER PAPERS READ ON THE OCCASION,

WITH

AN ACCOUNT OF THE PROCEEDINGS AT THE CELEBRATION.

BOSTON:
PRINTED BY ALFRED MUDGE & SON
34 SCHOOL STREET.
1876.

PREPARATORY PROCEEDINGS.

AT the close of preparatory lecture, July 3, 1874, the propriety and expediency of a centennial celebration of the church were considered. It was voted, unanimously, to commemorate the one hundredth anniversary of the organization of the church with appropriate services, and a committee of arrangements were appointed to whom the matter was intrusted.

At a meeting the next day, and at subsequent meetings, the committee fixed upon the 20th of October, 1874, for the celebration. They invited Quincy Blakely to prepare a historical discourse, Joseph Cook to give a historical sketch of the Sabbath School, Selden C. Willey to give a historical sketch of the Sacred Music Society, and William G. Brown to give some account of the several deacons of the church. Joseph Cook was designated for president of the day.

The committee, without unnecessary delay, issued the following circular, which was sent to all absent and former members of the church, so far as their post-office address could be ascertained, to several clergymen in the vicinity, and to the Baptist and Freewill Baptist Churches in town.

" CENTENNIAL.

" The Congregational Church in Campton, N. H., proposes to celebrate the one hundredth anniversary of its organization Tuesday, Oct. 20, 1874. Public services in the meeting-house, commencing at 10 o'clock, A. M.

" You are cordially invited to be present and participate in these commemorative exercises.

"QUINCY BLAKELY,
"JOSEPH COOK,
"WILLIAM G. BROWN,
"ERASTUS DOLE,
"THOMAS S. PULSIFER,
"CHRISTOPHER M. BARTLETT,
"MOSES C. DOLE,
" *Committee of Arrangements.*

"CAMPTON, N. H., Sept. 7, 1874."

The interior of the meeting-house was tastefully decorated with evergreens, cut flowers, and mottoes. On the wall in the rear of the pulpit was a large, heavily-wrought cross of evergreen, over which was the

name of the first pastor, "Church," with the date, "1774." On the left
were the names, "Chapin," "Webber," "Brown," "Hale"; on the
right, "Stone," "Beach," "Shedd," "Hadley"; directly under the cross
the name, "Blakely," with the date, "1874"; over the whole in a half
circle, "Our Pastors"; underneath the whole, in one line, "God is our
strength in all generations." On the front of the gallery was, "Praise
God in his sanctuary." These names and mottoes were all in evergreen,
evergreen festoons on the walls of the house, with hoops of evergreen
hung in the inverted arches. Bouquets of cut flowers were placed on
the table in front of the pulpit.

PROCEEDINGS AT THE CELEBRATION,

IT was a bright, mild, lovely day. Long before the hour for the exercises to commence had arrived the people began to assemble on the meeting-house green. Old friends, long separated, met and exchanged hearty greetings, recognizing often under the bowed form and gray hairs of age the bright, buoyant associate of years long since gone by. The young and some in middle life now for the first time became acquainted with some who had in former years been active in the service of Christ and in the maintenance of the institutions of religion here, and who had come back from their now distant homes to join in the festivities of this Centennial Celebration. A feeling of gladness seemed to pervade the hearts of all, from the octogenarian down to the child of two years.

When the bell struck for 10 o'clock, the cheerful chatting about things of former days ceased and the people assembled in the sanctuary. They were called to order by the president of the day, Joseph Cook, who in fitting terms bade them a joyful welcome, and announced in general the order of exercises, naming those who had been invited to prepare special papers for the occasion, and stating that he had invited Charles Cutter to perform the service asked of himself, viz. to prepare a historical sketch of the Sabbath School.

The exercises commenced with singing "Before Jehovah's awful throne" to the tune "Denmark." Rev. Dr. N. Bouton, of Concord, read Ps. 78: 1-7, Eph. 4: 1-13 and 3: 20-21. The 136th Psalm was read responsively, the pastor reading the first part of each verse and the congregation the last part, — "For his mercy endureth forever." Prayer by Rev. J. B. Hadley, a former pastor of the church. The 78th Psalm, "Let children hear the mighty deeds," was sung. Then followed the historical discourse by the pastor, during a pause in which a hymn was sung. A paper on the Deacons of the Church was presented by Dea. Brown; a historical sketch of the Sacred Music Society, by S. C. Willey, Esq.; a historical sketch of the Sabbath School, by Charles Cutter, Esq. After singing the doxology, J. Sharp, "Praise God from whom all blessings flow," the congregation took a recess for an hour, during which time they repaired to the Town Hall and partook of a bountiful collation, after a blessing had been invoked by Rev. F. W. Tolman, of the Baptist Church, Campton Village. After dinner, exercises were resumed in the meeting-house. Prayer was offered by Rev. William R. Jewett, sketches of piety and several letters from absent ones, were read, and short addresses made by Rev. Messrs. J. B. Hadley, N. Bouton, D. D., of Concord, William R. Jewett, of Fisherville, and Isaac Willey, of Pembroke, and Dea. Diadate Willey and David Bartlett, Esq.

The singing for the occasion was by the choir, led by J. C. Blair, with Warren Tucker and Gardiner Little as organists. Besides the pieces already named there were sung the 33d hymn, "The promises I sing," to the tune "Lenox;" "Antioch," " Confidence," "Concord," and " Northfield."

On motion of David Bartlett, seconded by Rev. Isaac Willey, voted to adjourn one hundred years for the celebration of the two hundredth anniversary of the organization of the church.

The closing prayer was by Dr. Bouton; benediction by Rev. Isaac Willey, after which the assembly dispersed with evident satisfaction and delight, feeling it was good to have been there, and that the celebration had in every particular met their most sanguine expectations.

HISTORICAL DISCOURSE.

It is pleasant, from our standpoint, to look back along the track of time to the organization of this church, whose one hundredth anniversary we this day celebrate, and note its history, speak of its achievements in the great work of the Master, its trials, its conflicts, its victories. For one hundred years has God had a people here. From Sabbath to Sabbath, and from time to time, have they assembled for his worship. These valleys and hills round about us have been made vocal with praise to our God and to our fathers' God. While one generation of believers after another have passed on into the spirit world, others have arisen to take their places and to enter into their work. And to-day the candle of the Lord is burning here; and may it please God to continue it through each succeeding generation, until generations shall be no more.

Frequently during the century have men and women stood up here, before God and angels, and publicly professed faith in Christ as their Saviour, and have entered into solemn covenant with God and his people. All the original members and many of their successors are to-day, we trust, singing the song of Moses and the Lamb in the kingdom of Heaven.

Isaac Fox and Winthrop Fox were the first to settle in Campton. Tradition fixes, with a good degree of probability, the date of their settlement in the spring of 1762. The town was originally granted to Gen. Jabez Spencer, of East Haddam, Conn., in the year 1761; but he died before the needful settlements were effected, and the title became invalid. A new charter was secured in 1767. The early settlers were from the southern part of Connecticut, near the mouth of the river by that name, and from the eastern part of Massachusetts, in the vicinity of Newburyport, including a few of the towns in the southern part of this State. They were men of true Puritan stamp, holding in high estimation the Bible and Christian institutions and schools of learning; hence, we find them at once making earnest efforts to secure these privileges for themselves and their posterity. Nathaniel Emmons — afterwards the celebrated Dr. Emmons — was the first candidate for settlement in the ministry here, and for a time it seemed probable that he would become the pastor of this people. But God had another field for him. The Congregational Church in Campton was organized June 1, 1774, in the dwelling-house of Nathaniel Tupper. Probably, said house was a log-house, standing near where the one recently occupied by John Hanaford stands, and which is now being torn down. We know not who, nor how many, constituted the church at its organization. No records of the church previous to 1800 are known to be in existence. It is quite probable that some, at least, of the original members were members of churches elsewhere before they came here. The membership must have been very small at the beginning, as the whole population of the town at that time could not have greatly exceeded one hundred and fifty.

In those days there was no ecclesiastical Society, as now, to provide for the support of gospel institutions, but the town, in its corporate capacity, made such provision just as they would provide for the support of schools.   At a legal town-meeting at the house of Col. Joseph Spencer, on Thursday, the seventh day of January, 1773, —

"Voted, Secondly, to Choose a Committee to procure a minister to preach the Next Summer. Voted, Ebenezer Taylor, Joseph Palmer, Samuel Cook, Be Chosen Said Committee. Voted, the Said Committee Have power to apply to any person or persons to provide a minister to preach in Said town three months the Next Summer, and to provide any Necessaries for Said Minister at the Cost of the Town."

This is the earliest town record on the subject we find, although it is probable they took action earlier than this. Several leaves from the first of the record book are missing. No report of the action of this committee is on record in the town book. Sept. 7, 1773, the town chose Benjamin Hickcox, Samuel Holmes, and Joseph Spencer a town committee to procure a minister to preach on probation for settlement, and defray all necessary charges. At a town meeting, Nov. 15, 1773, —

"Voted, that Capt. Benjamin Hickcox, as Being one of the Committee for the Town, Should procure, if May Be, a Minister to preach with us Next Summer, have him come at May, 1774."

It would seem that this committee negotiated with Mr. Selden Church, and made report. For at the annual town-meeting March 15, 1774, it was —

"Voted, that the Committee Shall apply to Mr Selden Church according to his proposals to preach two months with us. Voted, to Meet at the House of Col. Spencer, in Campton, the year Ensuing, for the purpose of public worship."

It appears that an arrangement was made with Mr. Church to preach two months, and that his labors were acceptable to the people. In the selectmen's warrant for town-meeting, to be holden May 26, 1774, we find, —

"Then and there, after a Moderator is chosen, to act on the following particulars: 1st. To See what Method the Town will come into and Defray the Charges which have arisen or May arise from Mr Church's preaching in Said Town. 2d. To See if the Town will Come into Some Method To Settle a Gospel Minister. 3d. To See if the town will Give Mr. Selden Church a Call for Settlement in Said town, and Choose a

Committee to treat with him as they Shall Receive orders from Said Town."

At this meeting, May 26, 1774, it was voted to raise eleven pounds, ten shillings, lawful money, a year for six years, and then to rise five pounds a year until it shall amount to seventy pounds, lawful money, which three ounces of silver amounts to one pound lawful money and is equally the same, for the salary and support of any minister that may appear to settle with us. Voted, to raise on grant one hundred and five pounds lawful money's worth in labor and provision at cash price for the settlement of a minister, to be paid in four years, one fourth part annually. Voted, Messrs. Benjamin Hickcox, David Perkins, and Joseph Spencer be chosen a committee to treat with Mr. Selden Church with regard to his settlement. Voted, Samuel Holmes, John Southmayd, and Gershom Burbank be chosen a committee to notes or bonds which are granted by the propriety for the support of a gospel minister in Campton, also to give sufficient bonds to the town to be left in the hands of the town treasurer. This committee were jointly and severally to come under bonds of five hundred pounds lawful money for surety to the town, — a careful provision against loss, surely. This action of the town doubtless had special reference to Mr. Church, although it was not restricted to him. The provision made was for the salary or yearly support of the minister, whoever he might be. We find, also, the following record, which may serve to explain what was meant by "settlement" in connection with salary: —

" Voted, that whereas the propriety of the town of Campton did, at a legal meeting of the proprietors on the 26th day of May, 1774, held at Campton aforesaid, vote and grant the sum of four pounds lawful money on each whole right, or proprietor's share of land towards the supporting of a gospel minister or ministers in said town, to be raised and applied in the manner and in the time therein mentioned; therefore, voted, that we acknowledge and receive the same as a full and complete satisfaction on the part and behalf of the propriety and lands in said Campton, towards settling and supporting a minister or ministers in said town, and also in consideration of said grant and vote acknowledge the proprietors and lands in said town to be free and clear from all and such like charges forever hereafter."

Having made provision for the temporal support of a minister, the town at once adopted measures to induct one into the pastoral office. At a legal town-meeting, at the house of Joseph Spencer, held on the 29th of August, 1774, —

" Voted, to give Mr. Selden Church a call for settlement in this place.

" Voted, that whereas, we agree that the ministerial office is of divine institution, for the Edifying and guiding of his church, and to continue to the end of the world; and they who are called to this office ought to be endowed with competent learning, ministerial gifts, as also with the grace of God, sound in judgment, not a novice in the faith and knowledge o the gospel, without scandal, of a holy conversation, and such as devote themselves to the work and service thereof; being thus agreed in the internal qualifications and outward acquirements of Mr. Selden Church, we hereby vote and call him to the pastoral charge of this town and congregation here, so long as he shall continue in the faith and order of the Gospel."

Then follows Mr. Church's reply: —

"CAMPTON, Aug. 29, 1774.

"To THE CHURCH AND SOCIETY IN CAMPTON:

"*Brethren and Friends*, — Having received your call to Settle with you in the work of the Ministry, I have taken the same into serious consideration; have Consulted and advised with my Friends, and I hope looked to God for Direction in this important affair. Considering the Great and Remarkable Union that appears in my favor, and Considering the prospect that arises from this and from Some other things, that I may Be a useful though an unworthy instrument in God's hands, of advancing the Redeemer's kingdom among you, by Doing good to Souls in this place: considering these things, I say, your Call appears to Be the Call of providence, and as such I can but think it my Duty to accept of it; and would hereby Signify my willingness to Devote My Self to your Service in the work of the Gospel Ministry. I trust you are not insensible that my usefulness among you, and our mutual comfort and Happiness in this relation, will depend, next to God's Blessing, on maintaining and Increasing that Union and love that Now appears, and on your and my own Mutual affection and Suitable work toward each other. I am Sensible that I am greatly insufficient for so important an Undertaking. I hope I Shall Engage in the Strength of Christ that is made perfect in weakness; for this purpose I Desire your prayers that I may have grace given me to walk as becomes the relation; that I may make it my Study to Show myself approved unto God, rightly Dividing the word of truth, and that I may so take heed to My Self and Doctrine and Continue in them, that in doing this I may both Save my Self and those that hear me.

"SELDEN CHURCH."

At this same meeting it was also, —

"Voted, to give Mr. Selden Church the cutting and hauling of thirty cords of wood yearly; which is to be cut about eight feet long, providing he shall find the same. This is done exclusive of his other salary, so long as he shall continue to be our minister."

The salary of Mr. Church, in the commencement of his ministry here, was seventy-six pounds and five shillings lawful money, and the cutting and hauling of thirty cords of wood. It should be remembered that the pound spoken of in the early history of the town was twenty shillings, and six shillings was equal to a dollar. A pound lawful money was equivalent to $3.33⅓. Mr. Church's salary was, therefore, equal to $254.16⅔, besides the cutting and drawing of thirty cords of wood. The time of payment fixed upon was the first day of October, annually, for the "settlement," and the first day of November, annually, for that part of the salary which was to be paid by the town. The meeting at which was voted a call to Mr. Church was adjourned to the tenth day of October, 1774, at which time the town voted, "that the inhabitants make a general entertainment for the ordination on free cost." Darius Willey, David Perkins, and Ebenezer Taylor were chosen a committee of arrangements. Also, voted, "that the rum and sweetening necessarily expended for the ordination shall be provided at the town's cost, and be equaled on the levy and collected by a rate in money as soon as may be." The town records give no account of the ordination services, nor of the fact of the ordination. But the manuscript sermon preached at the ordination is in the possession of Mrs. Ward, of Plymouth, a daughter of Mr. Church. The title-page is as follows: —

"A Sermon preached at the Ordination of the Revd. Mr. Selden Church to the Work and office of the Gospel Ministry in the Church and Town of Campton, Oct. 26, 1774. By Enoch Huntington, A. M., and Pastor of the first Church of Christ in Middletown. 'Arise, shine, for thy Light is come, and the glory of the Lord is risen upon thee.' Isaiah 60 : 1."

The text is Isaiah 35 : 1, 2, — "The wilderness and the solitary place shall be glad for them," etc. It is a sound and an appropriate sermon, written in a round, legible hand, and closes with "Amen, Finis." It is probable that the ordination services were at the house of Joseph Spencer, where the public worship on the Sabbath had been held during the summer.

The town, having settled a minister, proceed at once to secure a meeting-house. Dec. 5, 1774, the town "Voted to build a meeting-house 35 feet wide and 45 feet long." "Voted, to raise 65 pounds lawful money on the levy, or a rate to be taken 1775, in order to build said house." "Voted, Nathaniel Tupper, John Holmes, Daniel Wyatt, be chosen a committee to take the care and concern of building said house, that it be done prudently." This committee were instructed by the town to give the inhabitants a proper and reasonable opportunity to pay their rates for building the meeting-house in labor. At the same meeting it was voted, "That we hereby agree that the place now pitched upon for the meeting-house to stand is upon the hill north of Mr. Joseph Pulsifer's, and north of the saw-mill road, on the main road through the town, in the most convenient place as shall be agreed upon by the said committee appointed for building the same." This vote was made void a few months later and three "reputable" men from out of town, "Col. David Hobart. Dea. John Williby, and Mr. William Thornton, were chosen a committee to locate the house "; and a town committee of three were appointed to "represent, treat with, wait upon and entertain this locating committee, all at the cost of the town." This committee fixed upon the same place, or very nearly the same as that named by the previous committee, and it was accepted by vote of town March 21, 1775. At a meeting a week later the town voted to raise four pounds, ten shillings, lawful money, — about $15, — to purchase one acre and a half of land to set the meeting-house on. Nothing further, in this matter, seems to have been done, except to reconsider these votes, until September, 1775, when it was voted " that the spot for the meeting-house is agreed upon and pitched in the first original place that was agreed upon Dec. 5, 1774, which is on the hill north of Joseph Pulsifer's, north of the saw-mill road, on the main road leading through the town, on the farm of Col. Joseph Spencer." This place thus described must be on the hill back of this house in which we are now assembled and not many rods from it. But it does not appear that a meeting-house was built upon this spot or anything done in the matter other than to clear the land. All action by the town towards securing a meeting-house seems to have been suspended until Aug. 30, 1779, when they appointed Moses Baker, John Holmes, and Daniel Wyatt a committee to agree with Joseph Pulsifer for his dwelling-house for the use of the town. At an adjourned meeting, Sept. 13, 1779, it was voted to purchase Joseph Pulsifer's dwelling-house for the use of the town as agreed by the committee. This house stood a few rods northeast from where George H. Little now lives. The necessary changes were made therein, and now, more than five years after the organization of the church, they had for the first time a meeting-house, which was also used for town-meetings. This delay to secure a meeting-house was doubtless more on account of the disturbed condition of national affairs than for any lack of interest in gospel institutions among the people here. We must remember that during these years we, as a nation, were engaged in settling a somewhat serious difficulty with the mother country, which demanded the attention of all classes. And there seems also to have been at this time a feeling among those who resided on the west side of the Pemigewasset River that their convenience would not be met should the meeting-house be located on the spot which had been designated by the committee and accepted by the town. As early as 1775 the town voted " that the inhabitants on the east side of the Pemigewasset River have liberty to pitch, agree upon, and establish the place for the meeting-house of public worship, allowing the inhabitants on the west side of said river, in said town, to form themselves into a distinct parish, separate from the east side, when they shall think proper; and be paid back, when they so form themselves into such a parish, all the money they may or shall expend towards building the meeting-house on the east side of the aforesaid river, and also such part of, or their proportion of, the said money voted by the proprietors of Campton towards the support of the gospel in said town, as may appear to remain due from the proprietary agreeable to the vote of the proprietors, at the time the said west side so form into a parish." And in January, 1777, it was voted to establish a ferry over the river near where the

Blair Bridge is now, thus enabling those living on the west side the more conveniently to get to meeting, which was on the east side for several years. It appears that the inhabitants on the west side of the river were not entirely satisfied to have the meetings for public worship all on the east side. At the March meeting, 1786, it was voted "that the meetings shall be held for the present year on the west side of the river, at Mr. Samuel Cook's, one Sabbath in three, beginning on the east side." Mr. Cook lived near where Messrs. Bickford and Blaisdell now live. The meetings on the east side two thirds of the Sabbaths — as well as the town-meetings — were at the meeting-house. At the next annual town-meeting, March, 1787, a similar vote was passed, — public worship one third of the Sabbaths on the west side and two thirds on the east side. It appears that the meeting-house was then becoming unfit for public worship as well as its location objectionable. In the warrant for town-meeting to be held in the meeting-house January, 1788, we find, —

" 2. To see if the town will agree upon a spot of ground where to set a meeting-house. 3. To see what the town will do in regard to building a meeting-house."

At this meeting it was voted, " to set a meeting-house as nigh Mr. Isaac Fox's dwelling-house as the land will admit." Mr. Fox lived near where the tomb is now, near enough to the river, in the time of a freshet, to have his corn, which he had spread on his kitchen floor, in the ear, to dry, washed into the cellar through a trap-door which the water had opened. This vote was not carried out. At the March meeting the same year, 1788, " Voted, that the selectmen repair the meeting-house on the town's cost." It is not certain that the house was repaired, probably not. Three years later, April 14, 1791, the town voted " that public worship be held at the house of Mr. Isaac Fox for the future." Also, " Voted, that Moody Cook, Abel Willey, and John Southmayd be a committee to agree with Nathaniel Tupper, in exchange of houses to hold public worship in." In May following, the town voted to move the meeting-house on to the top of the hill east of Isaac Fox's dwelling-house. It appears that this vote was carried out, and the place to which the meeting-house was moved was several rods south of what is now the main entrance to the town cemetery. This settled the meeting-house question for about five years, during which time public worship and town-meetings were held in the meeting-house thus located; and by means of the ferry over the river near by, the people living on the west side of the river were tolerably well accommodated. After this, we find that the town-meetings were held at the Clothier's house, so called, which stood on the west of the Pemigewasset near the present bridge at Livermore Falls. An article in the warrant for town-meeting, to be held March 15, 1796, reads, " To see what the town will do with regard to building a meeting-house or houses." At this meeting it was " Voted, to build two meeting-houses, one on each side of the river, as shall be most convenient, and board and shingle the same; and the rest be done by the pews." This vote was reconsidered the 11th of April following. At a town-meeting March 20, 1798, the meeting-house was sold, at vendue, to Nathaniel Tupper, for $20. For a time public worship was held in private houses again.

Mr. Church's ministry with this people continued some eighteen years. He was dismissed in 1791, but continued to supply the pulpit for some time after. At a town-meeting, Oct. 15, 1792, it was voted to re-settle him in the gospel ministry, and Abel Willey, Samuel Holmes, Moody Cook, and Ebenezer Bartlett, Jr., were chosen a committee to give Mr. Church a call. But it does not appear that he accepted this call, although he remained in town until as late as 1795, and preached more or less or the time. This was the last effort on the part of the town to settle a minister. He is spoken of as a learned and godly man, sound in the faith, and a useful minister. His influence for good has been felt all through the century, and its force will not be spent, we trust, for centuries yet to come. He laid the foundation broad and deep; he carefully watched the workings of the Holy Spirit; was earnest to guard against any influence calculated to drive the Spirit away. It is said of him that at one time, when there were some indications of the Spirit's special presence here, — already working with power in Hebron, — on the morning of training-day he kindly remarked to a young man that he hoped nothing would be done that day to grieve the Spirit away. The remark was as an arrow from the quiver of God to the young man's heart. He carried his gun and knapsack all day; but he was, meanwhile, greatly exercised for his soul's salvation. He soon after became a Christian, and in after years, and until his death in 1844, a beloved and honored deacon of the Church; and his posterity down to the fourth generation are living Christian lives to-day.

Mr. Church's labors must have been arduous, coming here, as he did, a young, unmarried man, when the country was new, and probably not more than thirty families in town, and they scattered over quite a territory, which was divided by a bridgeless river. The deprivations to which he was subject were such as are usually incident to new settlements, and largely increased in consequence of the protracted War of the Revolution. During the first five years of his ministry here there was public worship in private dwellings. He remained unmarried until Oct. 14, 1779, when he married Miss Mary Baker. When the fact became generally known, the house-warming that followed was an occasion greatly enjoyed by the people, some pleasing reminiscences of which are related to-day. Mr. Church lived in a gambrel-roofed house where Dea. Brown's house now stands. Some of the people living at a great distance from the place of public worship, and who came to meeting either on foot or with ox-teams, were wont to think that his sermons would have been improved if they had been shortened, — no complaint with regard to the matter of them; it was to their length that objection was made. Some of the people once agreed that if he did not close by a special time they would take their hats and start for home; and they did. This is not so bad as a story told of a preacher in ancient times, before church clocks were in fashion, and when they measured time by the hour-glass: "He had exhausted his sand-glass, turned it, and gone through three fourths of another running; the congregation had nearly all retired, and the clerk, tired out, audibly asked his reverend superior to lock up the church and put the key under the door, when the sermon was done, as he (the clerk) and the few remaining auditors were going away."

Mr. Church must have been a man of sterling character, endowed with wisdom, and an earnest worker, to have been so successful through so long a pastorate amid such difficulties as he had to encounter. In 1795 he published a little work entitled " A Pocket-Mirror for Self-Excusers," an excellent book; it ought to be reprinted. Selden Church was born in East Haddam, Conn., Apr. 13, 1744; graduated at Yale College, 1765; studied theology with Rev. Enoch Huntington, of Middletown, Conn.; ordained in Campton, Oct. 26, 1774; dismissed, 1791; died in Northumberland, July 14, 1802.

After Mr. Church left town, there was no stated minister with this people until 1800. But during this period the people met regularly on the Sabbath for public worship, in meetings conducted by the deacons when no minister could be procured, and were fully attended. At this time, Dea. Evans, of Hebron, a godly and devoted man, occasionally came and visited from house to house, and assisted in conducting the meetings. They had no meeting-house and were without a pastor. About this time many of the families residing on the west side of the Pemigewasset River commenced going to Plymouth for their church privileges, and continued thus to do until the year 1824, when a meeting-house was built on the west side of the river.

In 1798 the church began preparations for building a meeting-house. The frame was put up in 1799; the house was finished in 1802. It cost $2,000. It stood in front of the old burying-ground, near the store now occupied by C. W. Cook. It had square pews, high galleries extending round on three sides, a high pulpit, a sounding-board above, and deacons' seats in front, facing the audience. The last Sabbath service in this house was Oct. 10, 1858. The house stood unoccupied, a relic of the past, until 1864, when the proprietors sold it at auction to G. W. Keniston, for $105. It was taken down in 1866, and the timber used in the construction of Cook's Hall, Plymouth. Peletiah Chapin was the first to preach in this house. He commenced his ministry here in 1800. He came from Newport here. He refused to be installed pastor, saying that he was like his horse, sure to break loose if he were tied, but would stand untied any length of time. He was a man of ability, a forcible and impressive preacher, but somewhat eccentric. In 1805 Mr. Chapin declared his dissent from the Congregational Church, and united with a Baptist Church in a neighboring town. Such was his influence that about one third of the members of the church gradually came into sympathy with him. He declined the invitation to continue his ministry in the parish. He held a separate meeting in town, which was attended by those who were in sympathy with him. There was some bitterness of feeling engendered. Many of those who sympathized with him were owners in the then new meeting-house, and claimed the privilege of occupying it a portion of the time. This claim was respected, and they occupied the meeting-house a part of the time, while the church held meetings in the school-house. After a while the Congregationalists purchased of those who avowed Baptist sentiments their interest in the meeting-house, and thus became sole owners of the house. The church was very much weakened by so many valuable members going off, but still held on and faithfully maintained the institutions of religion.

It appears that the confession of faith and covenant were revised about the commencement of Mr. Chapin's ministry. This creed is short and evangelical. This minute is found in the church records, immediately following the confession and covenant: " Apr. 13, 1800. Nathaniel Tupper and his wife, Jonathan Burbank and his wife, David Bartlett, Josiah Blaisdell, and Deborah Willey consented to the above confession, Rev. Noah Worcester being present; afterward Dea. William Baker and his wife and Dea. Wyatt did the same. May 25, Pelatiah Chapin and Joshua Rogers did own the same confession with the above." How long these individuals may have been members of the church, or how many of them, if any, were among the original members, we know not, neither do we know who had died or been dismissed previous to 1800. During the year 1800 Mary Willey, Sarah Cook, Moses Baker, Isaac Fox, Deborah Baker Joanna Bartlett, and Abigail Noyes were added to the church. In 1801 and 1802 Sarah Rogers, David Wooster, Ruth Southmayd, Olive Durgin, James Burbeck, and wife, Joseph Burbeck, Isaac Fox, 2d, Sarah Whitney, Tristram Bartlett, Abigail Pulsifer, and Martha Palmer were received into the church. From 1802 to 1807 the church records are very meagre, except the names of twenty-three children and the dates of their baptism. Rev. Daniel Staniford followed Mr. Chapin in the ministry here and continued a little over a year. He was not installed. The first record of his service was September, 1806, and the last, November, 1807. During this time the church adopted a new creed and covenant very much longer than those adopted in 1800, though perhaps no more orthodox, unless length is a feature of orthodoxy. The confession in 1800 expresses belief in inspiration; one God, the Creator; the doctrine of the Trinity; man's original righteousness; his fall; the depravity and entire ruin of the race; the atonement of Christ; the necessity of regeneration in order to salvation; in the resurrection, judgment, and life everlasting, either in happiness or misery. The confession adopted in 1807 is very much fuller, especially in its enumeration of the attributes of God. Mr. Staniford is spoken of as a man in feeble health, of considerable culture, an earnest worker. His labors were valuable in establishing the minds of the people in the doctrines of the Bible, and in giving stability to the church. He was a graduate of Harvard College in 1772. He was unmarried; born in Ipswich. After he left Campton lived in Sandown, where he died. For two years after Mr. Staniford closed his labors here the church was without stated preaching, but meetings were regularly held on the Sabbath, at which sermons were read. During this period, and at other times when the church had no minister, the ordinances of baptism and the Lord's Supper were administered by neighboring ministers. The name of Mr. Fairbank is of frequent occurrence in connection with such service. Rev. Messrs. Hovey, Worcester, Rankin, Sewall, Smith, and Spofford are also mentioned as performing these rites.

Dr. Kitridge, formerly a practising physician, supplied the pulpit a year, 1810. He was father of the late Judge Kitridge. He was paid, in part at least, in grain, and came from Canterbury for it with a two-horse team.

In February, 1812, Rev. John Webber, brother of President Webber of Harvard College, a native of Rowley or Byfield, Mass., a graduate of Dartmouth College in 1792, was installed pastor of this church. The day of the month is not recorded, nor are the doings of the council. It is remembered by some of the old people that the day was a bitter cold one, that the Rev. Ethan Smith of Hopkinton preached the installation sermon from the text, " Ye are the light of the world," and that Rev. Messrs. Carpenter, Fairbank, and Rolfe had parts in the services. Mr. Webber was regarded as a man well informed, a clear and forcible preacher. It is said that " a large proportion of his preaching pertained to the Abrahamic covenant, with frequent thrusts at the close communion system." He was not a very popular minister. After a pastorate of about three years he was, by advice of council, dismissed March 23, 1815. The record is, " After many conferences of the church with Mr. Webber, the pastor, from December, 1814, to the above date, March 15, 1815, respecting existing difficulties, the church and pastor then agreed to invite the pastors and delegates from our sister churches, Groton and Plymouth, to attend with us as an advisory council." The council was composed of Rev William Rolfe and Dea. Isaac Cheney, of Groton, Rev. Drury Fairbank and Dea. Asa Robbins, of Plymouth. After a full hearing they say in their "result," " There appeared no charges of the nature of moral evil or heresy alleged, either by the pastor or the church, against each other. But the council are of the opinion that the pastor has occasionally indulged himself in imprudent expressions, such as have tended to alienate the affections of the church and society towards him, and do not accord with the Scriptural caution to ministers, ' that they be harmless as doves.' We do not think that on the part of the church there has been that Christian faithfulness towards their pastor that would be desirable and which so happily tends to cement the union between pastor and church. On the whole, taking all circumstances into view, the smallness of support afforded the pastor, the little prospect of increase, and the hope that a separation may open the door for the church and society to be united in the speedy

3

re-settlement of the gospel ministry among them, the council are unan-imously agreed that it is expedient that the pastoral relation between the Rev. John Webber and the church in Campton be dissolved. And it is hereby dissolved." Mr. Webber went from here to Ohio, where he labored much as a missionary. Died at Carlisle, Ohio, Oct. 9, 1852.

The spiritual prospects of the church were now very dark. They were without a pastor, few in number, only six resident male members, and they somewhat advanced in life. There was much to discourage them. The young, of whom there were many in town, were given to worldly pleasures. But the Lord was better unto them than their fears; He is able to save by few or many. It is often the darkest just before day. In the fall and winter after Mr. Webber was dismissed, God poured out his spirit here in copious measure. There were about one hundred hopeful conversions. This was truly a most remarkable revival. To give any-thing like a complete history of it would occupy more time than is allotted for this discourse. The revival commenced when the church was with-out a minister. After the work commenced help was obtained. Mr. War-ren Day, a licentiate, who had studied theology with Prof. Shurtleff of Hanover, was employed to preach for a time, and his labors were signally blessed. As Mr. Day's health and strength began to fail under his exhausting labors, he made a protracted exchange with Dr. McKeen of Bradford, Vt., who labored here some three weeks, preaching almost every day during that time, at the meeting-house on the Sabbath and in school-houses or private dwellings during the week. He wrote in his diary, Monday, Feb. 5, 1816, " Left dear, blessed Campton for home. God has been working mightily among this people. Wonderful have been the displays of his grace and power in subduing the hearts of many unto the obedience of faith. He has appeared in his glory in building up Zion." Rev. Mr. Hovey of Piermont and Rev. Mr. Fairbank of Ply-mouth rendered important assistance in the good work. Zeal and fer-vency characterized many of the converts. God owned their efforts in behalf of their associates and neighbors. As they had been taught of the Spirit so went they forth to teach others, believing that " faith cometh by hearing, and hearing by the Word of God." The little band of faithful ones who had been steadfast in maintaining the worship of God on the Sabbath amid many discouragements, were now greatly rejoiced and strengthened. Their number was increased until the few became a host. Six young men, subjects of this revival, afterwards entered the ministry, — Christopher Marsh, Isaac Willey, Leonard Rogers, Daniel Pulsifer, George W. Elliott, and John Wooster. One of this number, Chris-topher Marsh, at the ordination of Worcester Willey in 1844, remarked, " Twenty-nine years ago at this time I was inquiring what I must do to be saved. The second Sabbath in January following I was one of thir-teen who in this house publicly professed Christ before the world. An interesting revival of religion was then in progress, which brought a large number into the church. From all my knowledge of that revival, its origin, its progress, and results, and from all the experience I have had in revivals in other places from that time to this, I am in the habit of thinking of the revival in this town in 1815-16 as the most precious and the freest from anything spurious or exceptionable of any revival that has fallen under my observation." There are those still living, members of this church, who were subjects of that revival, who have been accustomed to regard it as the most glorious, refreshing, the most remarkable revival they have ever known. They remember that twenty were struck under conviction when listening to one sermon preached by Mr. Day, from the text, " The harvest is past, the summer is ended, and we are not saved." If they could tell us, to-day, a tithe of what they remember of that revival, I am sure it would gladden all our hearts, and we should feel to pray the Lord of the harvest that he would in like manner appear and work among this generation.

The next minister was Rev. A. P. Brown, a native of Thornton, not a graduate of college; had studied theology with Dr. Wood, of Boscawen. Having labored here a short time in the fall of 1816, with great acceptance, he was called to the pastorate of this church, and was installed Jan. 1, 1817; sermon by Rev. Mr. Hovey, consecrating prayer by Rev. Mr. Ward, charge by Rev. Mr. Price, right hand of fellowship by Rev. Mr. Fairbank, charge to the people by Rev. Mr. McKeen. A general prosperity attended his ministry here, which continued five years. It was during his pastorate that the Congregational Society was incorporated; also, that the present parsonage lot was given to the Society by Col. Samuel Holmes, bounded as follows: " Beginning on the north side of Beebe's River, by the north end of the bridge across said river, on the road leading from my dwelling-house to the dwelling-house lately occupied by Jesse Willey, late of Campton, deceased; thence running northerly by the west side of the road, thirty-eight rods, to the road leading to the meeting-house; thence by the south side of the road leading to the meeting-house, forty-eight rods, to a stake and stones: thence southerly, by the line of land owned by the Hon. Arthur Livermore to Beebe's River; thence up and by said river to the bound first mentioned — containing, by estimate, twelve acres, be the same more or less." Mr. Holmes, although not a member of the church, also gave sixty dollars towards the erection of a house for a parsonage, and boarded the workmen while at work upon it. The old men of the parish undertook to build the house, and the young men the barn. When the whole was completed it was found that there was a debt of one hundred and fifty dollars. Col. Holmes said to the leading men of the parish, " You become obligated for one half of it, and you may put the other half to my account." The proposition was at once accepted. Mr. Brown was dismissed June 26, 1822. The council recommended him as an able and faithful preacher of the gospel. They say also, in their result, " Considering the pecuniary circumstances of Rev. Mr. Brown, the smallness of his salary, and the inability of the Society to give him the compensation which is necessary for his support, they judge it expedient that the pastoral relation between him and this church should be dissolved." After Mr. Brown was dismissed, and during the year 1823, Rev. A. Rankin, father of Dr. J. E. Rankin, now of Washington, D. C., preached for a time here and in Thornton on alternate Sabbaths. Both parishes moved in the matter to secure him for pastor, in which effort the people in Thornton were successful. At this time, 1823, stoves were first introduced into the meeting-house. How the people could endure it, to stay through all those long services in the severest weather with no fire in the meeting-house except what was carried in the small foot-stoves for the women, is a marvel to this generation; and yet such was the simple fact during the first forty-nine years of this church's existence. It was in 1821 that the first town-meeting was held in the meeting-house on the hill. At this meeting Rev. Mr. Brown offered prayer, the first prayer, says an octogenarian present here to-day, that he ever heard offered in town-meeting, but it was by no means the last one.

For a time after Mr. Brown was dismissed, it appears that the Society was weak in pecuniary ability, and their future prospects not flattering. Meetings, however, were regularly sustained on the Sabbath, preaching occasionally, and sermons read at other times. But a brighter day was soon to dawn upon them; some of the people residing on the west side of the Pemigewasset River, who commenced going to Plymouth for church privileges about the beginning of the present century, now came back, and, uniting with others, formed a second Congregational Society, and in 1824 built a meeting-house a little south of where J. C. Blair now lives, and removed their church relations to this church, — one church, two societies, two meeting-houses, services in each on alternate Sabbaths. May 23, 1824, Rev. Jonathan L. Hale, a native of Canaan, Ct., a graduate of Middlebury College, 1819, of Andover Seminary, 1822, who had been laboring in Colebrook in this State, under the auspices of the N. H. Missionary Society, for a year, having been ordained by the trustees of said Society, was invited to become the pastor of this church. He accepted, and was installed the twenty-third of the following month. Pres. Tyler, of Dartmouth College, preached the sermon; installing prayer by Rev. Mr. Fairbank; charge to the pastor by Rev. Mr. Ward; right hand by Rev. Mr. Farnsworth; address to the people by Rev. Mr. Burnham. The new meeting-house on the west side of the river was dedicated Feb. 23, 1825. Mr. Hale preached the sermon; text, "Holiness becometh thine house, O Lord, forever." A precious revival of religion followed, almost immediately, the dedication of the house. Some fifty or sixty were reckoned as converts, many of whom were heads of families. The present confession of faith and covenant were adopted by the church May 7, 1825. When the meeting was on either side of the river, the people residing on the other side were seriously incommoded in attending. The river could be forded a part of the time during the summer, and could be crossed on the ice in winter; but at times it was dangerous crossing. On one occasion, soon after service had commenced in the house on the west side, a man rushed into the meeting-house and cried out, "A man is drowning in the river!" whereupon service closed, temporarily, without the benediction, and with earnest effort the much-loved physician, Dr. Kimball, was soon rescued from the water. This and other like perils stimulated the people to build a bridge, which was done by private subscription, nearly opposite the present residence of J. C. Blair, in 1829, at a cost of $1,000, one tenth of which was contributed by Rev. Mr. Hale. For several years there seems to have been great unanimity and general prosperity in the church. Mr. Hale is said to have remarked "that his parish, made up of about forty families, promptly furnished him his salary, and contributed annually about four hundred dollars for the various benevolent objects of the day." Early in the year 1830 two brethren with the pastor commenced pleading unitedly for the Holy Spirit's influence to heal alienations among the brethren, to convict and convert sinners. They continued to meet weekly for an hour until June, 1831, when a protracted meeting of three days was held with good results. It is feared that the work of the Spirit was hindered somewhat by alienations existing among the brethren. The record is, "A number, about the time of the meeting and since, have indulged hope. Of the number, twenty have united with the church; others will, it is probable, at some future time when the church shall be in a proper state to receive members." At his own request Mr. Hale was dismissed by advice of a mutual council, April 18, 1832. Those who were personally acquainted with Mr. Hale speak of him as a consistent, devoted, useful man. He became settled the same year of his dismission from this church in Windham, Me. At the advice of his physician, he went South in October, 1834, to spend the winter. He died Jan. 15, 1835, on the Island of Skidaway, near Savannah, aged forty-four.

Rev. Benjamin P. Stone, D. D., a native of Reading, Vt., a graduate of Middlebury College, 1828, of Andover Seminary, 1831, was installed pastor of this church, June 12, 1833. Sermon by Rev. Mr. Boardman; installing prayer by Rev. Mr. Hobart; charge by Rev. Mr. Ward; fellowship of the churches by Rev. Mr. Punchard; address to the people by Rev. Mr. Blake; address to the children by Rev. Mr. Tappan. The time of Mr. Stone's settlement was limited by mutual contract to five years. He was a good scholar, a sound theologian, his sermons clear and strong, not an orator, a safe counsellor, a faithful pastor. During his pastorate, existing difficulties in the church were removed, harmony to a good degree restored, and general spiritual prosperity enjoyed. During this period the church resolved that a pledge of total abstinence from ardent spirits, as a drink, be hereafter a condition for admission into the church. Dr. Stone was dismissed Sept. 11, 1837, to accept a call to the secretaryship of the N. H. Missionary Society. He became also treasurer of the same Society, and treasurer and depositary of the N. H. Bible Society, and editor of the "Congregational Journal," and afterwards for a short time of the "Christian Reporter." After his dismissal from this church he occasionally supplied the pulpit for a longer or shorter time when they had no minister. His advice was frequently asked with regard to the choice of a minister and the settlement of difficulties between brethren. The last time he preached here was Aug. 8, 1869. Concerning the sermon, one of the congregation remarked, "The boys can't beat that." He died in Concord, Nov. 26, 1870, aged sixty-eight.

The next minister was Rev. Thomas P. Beach. He came from Wolfeborough here. He was installed Feb. 21, 1838. Sermon by Rev. Mr. Hall; installing prayer by Rev. Mr. Punchard; charge, Rev. Mr. Suthard; fellowship of the churches, Rev. Mr. Leach; address to the people, Rev. D. Pulsifer. Whatever harmony may have existed here when Mr. Beach commenced his labors, his pastorate of three and a half years was emphatically a stormy one. The church records and the proceedings of the council with reference to his case are sufficient to make quite a volume, though it would be painful to read it. The council that dismissed him, Aug. 19, 1841, withdrew fellowship from him and advised his excommunication from the church, which was soon after done. From our standpoint, with a knowledge of some things that transpired, it is a wonder that he should ever have been called to the pastorate of this church, or that he should have been retained so long as he was. Writes one who was a member of the council that ordained him, and also of the one that dismissed him, in substance, as follows: " Mr. Beach was a terrible curse to the parish. It was always unaccountable to me how such a church as Campton was should have been deluded into a liking for him. The council, with great hesitation, consented to ordain him, and I have always blamed myself for taking any part in it; for he was not only destitute of the necessary papers, but he was unsound, or utterly ignorant, on some important points of doctrine. When the council were alone, we discussed the question, whether we ought to ordain him, until the people were out of all patience. After his dismissal he went about the country preaching and lecturing wherever he could, and going into places of worship and interrupting religious services by his ungracious tirades. Anti-slavery was his hobby; but anti-Bible, anti-Sabbath, anti-church, anti-religious rites and ordinances were his topics. It is a miracle that Campton church was not broken up by this deluded man. As it was, it barely escaped destruction; and if it had not possessed a measure of strength which very few other churches in the State had, its entire ruin would have been effected." A few months before he was dismissed, charges were preferred against him, before the church, which were sustained. At this time he abandoned the church, or, at least, the majority, as a band of miscreants, and proclaimed in a written communication his withdrawal of fellowship, renounced the pulpit and his own ordination; denounced the institutions of the church, of the Sabbath, and the ministry, together with all the several benevolent associations which are sustained by the church; denied the inspiration of the Scriptures. He was ready of speech and plausible; had a strong influence over an audience. He carried with him about a third part of the members of the church. Who can estimate the amount of evil occasioned by such a career? Much of this sad history will, doubtless, ever remain unwritten. But with all these evils before us, we find great relief in the hope that Mr. Beach, in after years, while residing in the State of Ohio, on reviewing his career in Campton, saw things in a different light; his views and feelings underwent a great and desirable change. It is said that more than once he remarked to his wife, in speaking of what he had said and done in Campton, "It does seem as though I must have been crazy." It is thought that his sudden death alone — which occurred in 1846 — prevented his communicating with this church, and endeavoring to do what he could to undo the evil that followed his erratic course here.

The condition of affairs when Mr. Beach left must have been anything but agreeable, and the prospect not very favorable for securing another pastor; and still the pulpit was not long vacant. Rev. Charles Shedd, a native of Rindge, a graduate of Dartmouth College in 1826, who had been for several years a teacher in Kimball Union Academy, and at New Ipswich, was called to the pastorate of this church. He was ordained pastor at the west meeting-house March 24, 1842. Sermon by Rev. B. P. Stone, D. D.; ordaining prayer by Rev. Mr. Hobart; charge by Rev. Mr. Ward; address to the people by Rev. Mr. Benson. Mr. Shedd was in many respects specially qualified for the very arduous and difficult work before him. He was regarded by his brethren in the ministry as a positive character, a sound theologian, an excellent sermonizer, and a decided disciplinarian. During his ministry the knife was freely used in severing the limbs that were thought to be diseased. Twenty-one were excluded from the church as the direct consequence of the defection occasioned, as was supposed, by the previous pastor. Several of these were afterwards restored. The hymn-book we now use — Church Psalmody — was introduced July 5, 1844. In 1853, there was a revival of religion of considerable power. The pastor wrote, "At the communion the first Sabbath in January, 1853, four were admitted to the church; it was a solemn season, never to be forgotten. The work then began with power. The Tuesday following was the day appointed for the pastoral visit; one hundred assembled, nearly all of them youth; the Holy Spirit was there; convicted sinners were there. In the evening a few remarks were made touching the present religious interest; it seemed like Pentecost; it was literally a Bochim; some sank upon their seats overwhelmed with emotion, and were unwilling to leave the house till they were conversed and prayed with. They came again at an early hour the next morning and found peace. The work proceeded with great stillness, and was supposed at the time to embrace sixty or seventy persons. Twenty-seven have united with this church, several with other churches, and others have yet made no profession." The interest continued about two years; meantime the church were accustomed to observe days of fasting and prayer occasionally, and invariably with good results. Mr. Shedd's pastorate continued between sixteen and seventeen years. He was dismissed Oct. 1, 1856, the connection to close immediately after the first Sabbath in November. The council earnestly recommended that the church and Society pay Mr. Shedd the sum of $200 in addition to the salary to which he was legally entitled. This recommendation of the council was carried out. A large majority of the church seem to have been his warm friends, while a few were as decidedly his opponents. Soon after he closed his labors with this people he went to Minnesota, where he still continues to labor in the gospel ministry. He visited Campton in 1865, and was cordially received by all classes. He preached on the Sabbath and also presided at the communion table.

Rev. James B. Hadley, a native of Goffstown, a graduate of Amherst College, in 1833, of Andover Seminary in 1836, succeeded Mr. Shedd. He was installed Oct. 13, 1858; sermon by Dr. Chickering; installing prayer by Rev. Mr. Sargent; charge by Rev. Mr. Conant; right hand by Rev. Mr. Boutwell; address to the people by Dr. Stone. In the forenoon of the same day this house in which we are now assembled, which is essentially the one built in 1824 on the west side of the river, but which had been taken down and removed to this place, was dedicated. Mr. Hadley preached the sermon, text, Lev. 19, 130, " Ye shall keep my Sabbaths and reverence my sanctuary." Mr. Hadley commenced his labors here the second Sabbath in May, previous to his installation, under very favorable auspices, — the congregation no longer obliged to worship in two meeting-houses, one on each side of the river, in each on alternate Sabbaths, as they had done for thirty-four years. This house was in process of reconstruction, and when completed the excellent organ we now have was placed in it, Mrs. Sarah Little, of Newbury, Mass., contributing $100 towards it. The new bell, a present to the Society from Sylvester Marsh, now of Littleton, a new chandelier, pulpit-lamps, and lamps for the orchestra, presented by George W. Wyatt, of Somerville, Mass.; the pulpit chairs, presented by Messrs. Merrill and Morrison, of Chelsea, Mass.; the pulpit Bible, a gift from Dr. B. P. Stone; the pulpit, sofa, table, carpets, and blinds, donated by the Ladies' Sewing Circle, were all arranged in their proper places. Harmony was restored among the members. Many who had long indulged a hope that they were subjects of renewing grace came forward and publicly professed faith in Christ. Others surrendered themselves to the rule and reign of Christ and became members of his visible church. A general spiritual prosperity prevailed. After a harmonious and useful pastorate of five years, Mr. Hadley was, by advice of council, dismissed May 19, 1863. He continues to reside among us, an active and exemplary Christian and an excellent parishioner, preaching occasionally in this and other pulpits in the vicinity.

The War of the Rebellion made inroads upon this church. Four young men, Cyrus Burbeck, Charles H. Willey, Hermon C. Stickney, and Henry D. Wyatt, at the call of their country, engaged therein, two of whom did not live to return. Cyrus Burbeck died at Chicago, Aug. 7, 1863, on his way home from the war; Charles H. Willey died July, 1863, near New Orleans. The loss of these two active young men was severely felt; Cyrus Burbeck had been the efficient clerk of the church for several years. Eight or ten others, members of the congregation and Sabbath School, were also in the war.

Rev. Quincy Blakely, a native of Pawlet, Vt., a graduate from the U. Vt., 1854, and Union Theological Seminary, 1857, preached here three Sabbaths in May, 1863; commenced stated labor January following; was installed pastor of this church, June 29, 1864; sermon by Rev. George B. Tolman; installing prayer by Rev. B. P. Stone, D. D.; charge to the pastor by Rev. J. B. Hadley; right hand by Rev. Henry A. Hazen; address to the people by Rev. William R. Jewett. Of his fitness for the work or success therein, it becometh not me to speak in this presence. And the history of this church during the last decade is so familiar to you all that it need not be rehearsed at this time. Suffice it to say, that great unanimity and harmony have prevailed.

I have thus hastily and very imperfectly sketched the history of this church during the one hundred years of its existence, an organization whose centennial anniversary antedates the centenary of our Republic. We inquire, What has been the occasion of its strength and of its perpetuity; what type of piety has prevailed; what has been its reputation among the churches? The occasion of its strength is not to be found in its numbers. It has never been large, and at times it has been reduced to a mere handful. It is not to be found in its wealth, for of this it never had much to boast of. It is not to be found in the geographical position of its sanctuary, for that is very unfavorable, considering the development of business in other parts of the town and in adjoining towns, to which many of our citizens go for trade, and for social and religious privileges. No, the source of the strength and the occasion of the perpetuity of this church is in that which is far higher, deeper, broader, and more enduring than any or all of these things. The membership have been rooted and grounded in the doctrines of the Bible. They have endeavored to build " upon the foundation of the apostles and prophets, Jesus Christ himself being the chief corner-stone." They have believed in God, in Jesus Christ; in man's original righteousness, and yet that he fell from that high and holy estate, and is by nature depraved, and will be forever lost unless renewed by the Holy Ghost, through sanctification of the truth and belief in the Son of God; in an unlimited atonement for sin, and " that whosoever believeth on the Son hath everlasting life; and he that believeth not the Son shall not see life; but the wrath of God abideth on him."

On a certain time, when some people more zealous than wise, perhaps, were holding meetings in the vicinity, at which Congregationalists were derided, among other things said, it was reported and believed that a well-known person prayed that the doctrine of election might be taken

4

out of the Bible. But the church paid no attention to these things, steadily held on their way, believing in God's sovereignty and in the perseverance of the saints. Our fathers not only believed the truths of the Bible, but they taught them to their children; they talked of them when they sat in their houses, when they walked by the way, when they lay down and when they rose up; they believed in the promises of a covenant-keeping God, that he would be a God unto them and to their seed after them. Our fathers were a Bible-reading and a Bible-loving people. Preaching that was not in harmony with the teaching of the Bible they would not accept, and they would be their own judges whether it was in harmony with the Bible or not. They believed that God works for the salvation of men and for the furtherance of his kingdom through the ordinary means of grace as well as through the extraordinary; hence they have endeavored to maintain religious service on the Sabbath continually, with the regular ministry when practicable, at other times by temporary-paid supplies, — believing that the laborer is worthy of his hire, — and when no minister could be procured, the deacons conducted the meetings, and a sermon was read. These meetings were fully attended; thus the people were kept together and never lost the habit of attending religious worship. While they have preferred the faith and order of the Congregational Church, they have freely co-operated with other denominations in the benevolent operations of the day; dismissing members to and receiving from other Evangelical churches, their ministers exchanging with those of any Evangelical denomination. This people have been a benevolent people, giving of their men and of their money to the work of the Lord. This, too, is a source of strength and ground of perpetuity. They have been enriched by what they have *given* rather than by what they have *retained*. Though they have not aimed to corrupt their ministers with riches, they have given generously of their substance to the various benevolent objects of the day. This has been one of those churches whose benevolent contributions compare favorably with the salary of their own minister, as well as with their inventory of property. The aggregate of the inventory of the members of this church, as found in the selectmen's book for the current year, is $34,632. To this might be added $8,362, as the inventory of others who regularly contribute for the support of gospel institutions, though not members of the church; and yet the charitable contributions of this church and Society for the last conference year was $423.96. And with business-like promptness do they pay their minister's salary. But they are not the least impoverished by giving. Usually those who have given the most liberally have enjoyed the greatest prosperity. They have given from principle, and have taught their children to give also. They have given men, too. There have been raised up and sent out from this church into the ministry ten young men, — Isaac Willey, Christopher Marsh, George W. Elliott, Daniel Pulsifer, Leonard Rogers, John Wooster, John Clark, Austin Willey, Worcester Willey, Samuel Hopkins Willey, eight of whom were natives of Campton. One other, Leonard Willey, had the ministry in view, but died while pursuing his studies at Williams College. Eight of these ten are still living. Some of them are present here to-day and will speak for themselves. This church has given not only money and men to help in the evangelization of the world, but has occasionally given the time of its own pastor to supply in destitute churches in the vicinity, or where the minister was disabled by sickness. I quote a single record, "The church voted that their pastor be requested to preach four Sabbaths in the destitute places within the county in the course of the year, provided the societies acquiesce."

This church has had a good reputation abroad. Writes one who was conversant with affairs here forty years ago, "There was not a church in the county that sustained a higher character for soundness in the faith, promptness in every good work, stability and reliability and Christian benevolence." Another, whose acquaintance with this people commenced in 1844, writes, "I now recall very distinctly and with admiration these impressions, viz. that they were an intelligent, Christian people, that they would not knowingly allow anything to stand between them and the truth as it is revealed. Last and not least, they have made religion a *business*."

This church by no means claims perfection for itself. It has made sad mistakes; it has many imperfections. It has to-day, and perhaps always has had, members not distinguished for Christian activity, — sort of silent members. The type of piety prevailing may not always have been the most desirable, — sometimes rugged and resolute rather than winning and gentle.

The office-bearers of the church are not here specially singled out, as they are to be remembered in a special paper. The Sabbath School and Sacred Music Society are also to be noticed in special papers. But there is another organization which is so intimately connected with the life and prosperity of this church, and which has been so fruitful of good works, that it must not fail of mention at this time, — the Ladies' Missionary Association, in its two departments, foreign and home. Its foreign department was organized more than thirty years ago, and has not in a single instance failed of holding its annual meeting for the election of officers, nor has it failed to make its annual contribution to the American Board, or, within a few years, to the Woman's Board. The home department is called the Cent Society. The officers and collectors are the same for each department. Their method of collecting funds is briefly this: They annually appoint collectors in different districts, who call upon all the ladies of the congregation, old and young, at their homes, in the autumn, for contributions to the foreign work, and in the early summer for contributions to the home work. This method is still heartily approved after so many years of trial.

Could we, at this closing up of the first century of this church's existence, have spread out before us, so that we could all take it in, all the good that has been accomplished through this instrumentality, the whole number converted, the happy influences exerted, how our hearts would be made to rejoice. Have we not reason for devout thanksgiving to God that the record is so fair? But then, again, could we know how many have passed from earth away, from among this people, unrenewed, who might, if the members of this church had been as faithful as they ought to have been, have become partakers of the great salvation, our hearts would be sad. While to-day we rejoice because of the great good accomplished, have we not reason to humble ourselves because of remissness in duty?

Let us imitate the virtues of our fathers, avoid their mistakes, and enter upon the work of the coming century with a firm resolve that we, each in his or her place, will be earnest for the Master, and seek to honor him by a more entire consecration of all that we have and are to his service.

MEMBERS OF THIS CHURCH WHO HAVE ENTERED
THE MINISTRY.

Isaac Willey, born in Campton, Sept. 8, 1793; graduated at Dartmouth College, 1822; studied theology with Pres. Tyler, and Profs. Shurtleff and Haddock of Dartmouth; ordained Jan. 18, 1825 pastor at Rochester, *1826.* 1825–1834; agent New Hampshire Missionary Society, 1834–1837; pastor at Goffstown, 1837–1853; secretary and agent American Bible Society for New Hampshire, 1853–1875; resides at Pembroke.

Christopher Marsh, born in Campton, Aug. 4, 1794; graduated at Dartmouth College, 1820; studied theology with Rev. Asa Rand, Gorham, Me.; ordained June 4, 1823; pastor at Sanford, Me., 1823–1827; pastor at Biddeford, Me., 1828–1831; secretary and general agent of Massachusetts Sabbath School Society for a time; pastor at West Roxbury, Mass., 1837–1850; resided at Jamaica Plain a few years; returned to Sanford, Me., August, 1858, where he died in the midst of his labors, June 30, 1859.

George W. Elliott, born in Thornton, Sept. 18, 1796; united with this church on profession, Aug. 18, 1816; studied at Meriden, N. H., and Andover, Mass.; graduated at Auburn Theological Seminary, 1824; installed at Lenox, N. Y., February, 1825; pastor at Lenox, 1825–1837; pastor in Illinois, 1837–1850; missionary in Milwaukee, Wis., 1851, where he now resides.

Daniel Pulsifer, born in Campton, Sept. 26, 1796; studied theology with Rev. B. P. Stone; ordained Jan. 23, 1835; preached five years in Hebron and Groton; pastor ten years at Danbury; preached in Vermont several years, and afterwards at Enfield and Dorchester; resides at Danbury.

Leonard Rogers, born in Campton, April 13, 1797; graduated at the Theological Seminary, New Brunswick, N. J., 1832; pastor in Western New York several years; preached also in several places in Wisconsin and in Illinois; present residence, Crystal Lake, Ill.

John Wooster, born in Campton, May 23, 1798; united with this church Jan. 23, 1816; ordained elder in Methodist Episcopal Church at West Windsor, Vt., Aug. 10, 1834; preached a year in each of the following places: Kingston and Loudon, N. H., Cabot and Plainfield, Vt.; was dismissed from the Methodist connection and united with the Caledonia (Vt.) Association, Oct. 14, 1839; acting pastor in Concord, Vt., 1841 and 1842; pastor, Granby, Vt., 1843–1858; died at West Burke, Vt., Dec. 4, 1873.

John Clark, born in Haverhill, June 25, 1800; united with this church on profession, Oct. 2, 1825; studied theology with Rev. George Punchard; ordained Jan. 23, 1835; preached in Wilmont and Danbury, 1835–1842; in Burke, Vt., 1842–1854; in Bridgewater, 1855; in Bristol, 1856–1857; resides in Plymouth.

Austin Willey, born in Campton, June 24, 1806; graduated at Bangor Theological Seminary, 1837; editor "Herald of Freedom," 1839–1856; ordained at Anoka, Minn., 1858, where he preached for a time. On account of ill health, gave up preaching; has been engaged in literary pursuits to some extent; resides at Northfield, Minn.

Worcester Willey, born in Campton, Sept. 1, 1808; graduated at Williams College, 1835; at Andover Theological Seminary, 1840; teacher for a time at Ashby, Mass., and Plymouth, N. H.; preached at Wellfleet, Mass., and Hardwick, Vt.; missionary among the Cherokee Indians, 1844–1869; now at work for the Massachusetts Bible Society; resides in Andover, Mass.

Samuel Hopkins Willey, born in Campton, March 11, 1821; graduated at Dartmouth College, 1845; at Union Theological Seminary, N. Y., 1848; ordained, November, 1848; pastor Howard Presbyterian Church, San Francisco, Cal., 1850–1862; Vice-Pres. of College of California, 1862–1870; pastor of Congregational Church, Santa Cruz, Cal., 1870. — Leonard Willey, born in Campton, Aug. 29, 1799; had the ministry in view, but died August, 1824, in Williamstown, Mass., while a member of Williams College.

THE DEACONS.

BY DEA. WILLIAM G. BROWN.

"And the apostles said, Wherefore, brethren, look ye out among you seven men of honest report, full of the Holy Ghost and wisdom, whom we may appoint over this business, — but we will give ourselves continually to prayer and to the ministry of the Word."

THE brethren acted on this injunction, and thus early in the Christian Church men were appointed to the office of deacons, whose particular work *then* was to look after the poor of the church, to disburse its charities, and to help in its secular interests as well as its spiritual, thus enabling the apostles and the ministers who were to follow them to attend more fully to their legitimate work, that of prayer and preaching.

Among our Congregational churches this office has always been recognized, and generally our churches have had the office filled, — sometimes having two persons to officiate as deacons, sometimes four, and in larger churches, six, and even eight.

The church, whose one hundredth anniversary we to-day celebrate, has had from its earliest history acting deacons. At *no* time has it been without *one*, and for nearly all the time has it had *two*, and sometimes, as at the present, three deacons to represent it.

It appears that Wm. Baker was the first chosen deacon of this church. He was in town in 1777, came from Epping; he was probably here earlier than that date, for at that time (1777) we find him a delegate to the first convention for the formation of a State government, held at Concord. He was a man of known, decided Christian character ever after he came to town. He continued in office as deacon till he died, Nov. 28, 1814, aged seventy-nine years, having served the church as deacon for nearly or quite thirty-eight years. He lived on the farm now owned by S. N. Stickney, and known as the "town farm."

Daniel Wyatt was the second chosen deacon of the church, but it is probable he was chosen about the same time, if not at the same meeting, in which Deacon Baker was chosen, for we find that he came into town in 1769, earlier than did Deacon Baker. He was from Newburyport. As he was here at the time the church was organized, it is but natural to suppose he might be chosen at the same time and place, and another fact bearing on this point is that the neighboring churches were in the practice of having two deacons; but Deacon Baker being the older man, and perhaps a little more conspicuous in town affairs, *might* have been *chosen* first and so *called* the first deacon. He was deacon for more than forty years. He died in 1821 at an advanced age, probably nearly ninety years. He lived where Daniel Wyatt now lives. He was known as the " Honest Miller " for more than forty years, and ground the grain for the families in all this region. His mill was at the " Livermore Falls," so called, and he daily walked to and from his mill, a mile and a half, as regularly as the day returned. Every man and every boy knew Deacon Wyatt, — knew him as the *miller*, knew him as the faithful, sincere *Christian*. Often did each boy, and man too, as he came to the mill with the load upon the horse's back, receive a kind word, a good suggestion, or an earnest appeal. He was a man of *decided* religious character. His religious life commenced under the preaching of Whitefield, and was maintained with unusual integrity to its close.

It is not known at what time Deacons Bartlett and Wooster were chosen, as our church records do not go back further than the year 1800; but in 1801 they accepted the office to which they had been previously elected. In 1807 Deacon Wooster embraced what was then termed " close communion views," left the church, and joined the Baptists. He was probably deacon about thirteen years. He was a good man. After Deacon Wooster left the church, Deacon Bartlett was the only acting deacon for several years, nearly nine, for we find that Deacon Burbeck was appointed to that office in 1816, and Deacon Wooster left in 1807, making nine years between his leaving and Deacon Burbeck's appointment. Deacon Burbeck died March 17, 1844, aged eighty-one years, having held the office twenty-eight years.

Deacon Bartlett died Aug. 31, 1844, aged eighty-three years, having been deacon nearly fifty years.

There have been times when this church has been without a minister for months together. During such intervals religious services were conducted by the deacons and other leading members of the church. These were called " Deacon's Meetings." These Sabbath services were encouraged and attended constantly by the leading families of the town. This, to us, is a fact of great importance, and one which ought not to be overlooked. There was a principle about it; God's worship on the Sabbath and in his house must be maintained. This was done by our fathers, minister or no minister; and would that the present generation were as wise and sincere and conscientious as were our fathers.

Deacons Baker, Wyatt, Bartlett, and Burbeck were held in high esteem for the part they took in these services; for it required much care and labor to procure and select suitable discourses, to read them, and to perform the other services in the appropriate manner in which they were performed. This, from his situation in the parish and from his qualifications, devolved much on Deacon Bartlett. To no other man has this church been so much indebted in all its interests as to him for more than forty years of its history.

I have just read several letters of his to his grandchildren in Lowell, when he was more than eighty years old; and in them all is expressed an earnest desire, especially for their spiritual welfare. In one of them, and at its close, are the following words: "Were I acquainted with Mr. Blanchard (then pastor) I should wish to send him my respects and entreat him to be faithful unto death." In one of his letters, written in 1842, when eighty-one years old, he closes thus: " Now may the blessing of God rest on you and make you blessings here in time, and abundantly prepare you for admittance into the kingdom of heaven, where you will go no more out forever. Pray for your old grandfather. Farewell! Farewell!" In the same year he closes another thus: "Now, dear grandchildren, I bid you farewell. Be faithful unto death"; and then says in a postscript, "It is painful to sit long in writing; I have yet another to write to your Aunt Moody." In another letter he says, "I have no greater joy than to hear that my grandchildren are walking in the truth." I have quoted these extracts from his letters to show how intent his heart was for the spiritual prosperity of his relatives and others. Truly, he loved Zion and her gates.

In 1826 Diadate Willey was chosen to the office of deacon. Deacons Willey and Burbeck served as deacons in the church together till 1844, when, after the death of Deacon Burbeck at that date, John Chandler was chosen to take his place in May, 1844. Deacon Chandler died March 11, 1856, aged fifty-eight years, having served the church twelve years.

In October following Deacon William Colby, who had been a deacon in a Vermont church and was living here, was chosen to fill the office which had been made vacant by the death of Deacon Chandler. In 1859 he moved to the West, and a year or two after died in Chicago. He was deacon of this church about three years. For nearly two years after Deacon Colby left, Deacon Willey was the only acting deacon.

In June, 1859, W. G. Brown and Jason Cook were both chosen as deacons, and both declined. In March, 1861, W. G. Brown and Jason Cook accepted the office to which they had previously been chosen.

Deacon Cook died March 3, 1871, aged fifty-one years, having been our faithful deacon ten years. Of Deacon Cook's *worth* I need not speak. The members of *this* church *knew* him, and knew his worth. His memory is cherished by us. I think it may be truly said of him that he was ever ready to do *his* part in every enterprise or benevolent work that came before the church.

In this connection, it will be proper for your speaker (and it certainly gives him great pleasure to be permitted) to say that during the ten years he was permitted and privileged to be associated with him as a brother deacon in this church, that our relations and associations and all our intercourse together were of the most friendly kind, and that our feelings, views, and actions seemed at all times to harmonize.

In July, 1871, Ezekiel Hodgdon was chosen to take the place of Deacon Cook.

5

Deacon Willey, Deacon Hodgdon, and Deacon Brown are the present deacons of the church. Deacon Willey has been the deacon of this church forty-eight years, Deacon Brown thirteen, and Deacon Hodgdon three.

Deacon Willey is our senior deacon, but on account of age and infirmity seldom meets with us or officiates as deacon. His presence with us is always greeted with pleasure.

From the foregoing, we learn that this church has had eleven regularly chosen deacons, viz. Baker, Wyatt, Bartlett, Wooster, Burbeck, Willey, Chandler, Colby, Brown, Cook, and Hodgdon. Of those who have lived, done their work, and *died*, I think it may be truly said, they were *good* men, and did their work *faithfully* and *well*, and have, we doubt not, entered upon their reward. And of the three that remain, it well becomes us each to ask, Has *their* mantle fallen, or shall it fall upon us?

THE SACRED MUSIC SOCIETY.

BY S. C. WILLEY.

VERY little can be said in relation to sacred music here, previous to the organization of the Campton Sacred Music Society in 1814. But as music has always been considered a very important part of divine worship, I think it was attended to at an early day after the planting of this church. I have been informed that as early as 1795 to 1797 a singing school was held at Col. Samuel Holmes', taught by King George, of Plymouth, which improved the singing very much; there was one, also, taught by Eliphalet Blaisdell. When the present century commenced it found us with very good church music. In the spring of 1814, Dr. Robert Morrison came into town. He was a lover of music and a pleasant singer. He proposed the organization of a musical Society, which was organized July 5, 1814, by electing the following board of officers, viz. Dr. Robert Morrison, president; Israel Spencer, vice-president; William Rogers, clerk; Isaac Willey, treasurer; Diadate Willey, James Burbeck, and David Bartlett, Jr., Standing Committee. May 27, 1816, Campton Musical Society met, agreeable to the constitution, and passed the following vote: *Voted*, that the Campton Musical Society be incorporated into a body to be known by the name of the Campton Sacred Music Society. Date of incorporation, Dec. 27, 1816; total number or members at this date, forty-five. Agreeably to the foregoing act of incorporation, a meeting was legally warned and holden Dec. 27, 1816. Chose Isaac Willey, Jr., Scribe, and proceeded to make choice of the following officers, viz. Moses Baker, Esq., president; Joseph Pulsifer, Jr., vice-president; Robert Morrison, chorister; Israel Spencer, first assistant chorister; Diadate Willey, second assistant chorister; William Rogers, clerk; David Bartlett, Jr., treasurer. Chose Rev. Amos P. Brown, Moses Baker, Esq., and Robert Morrison, a committee to draft By-Laws for the well-ordering and regulating the concerns of said Society.

The choristers, from the organization of the Society to the present time: Dr. Robert Morrison, to the time of his death, July 6, 1819, aged twenty-eight; David Bartlett, Jr., 1820 to 1828; Nathaniel Spencer, 1829; William H. Blair, 1830; J. C. Blair, 1831 to 1836; Nathaniel Spencer, 1837 to 1838; J. C. Blair, 1839; Nathaniel Spencer, 1840; J. C. Blair, 1841, to the time of his death, Oct. 29, 1864, having served as chorister thirty years; Joseph C. Blair, son of J. C. Blair, 1865 to the present time, — six choristers for sixty years.

The assistant choristers have been, Israel Spencer, Nathaniel Spencer, Diadate Willey, E. B. Morrison, David Bartlett, William H. Blair, Eliphalet Blaisdell, Austin Willey, William Rogers, Daniel Wyatt, Theodore Palmer, Davis Baker, Jr., Ebenezer Burbank, Gardiner Spencer, Henry Little, Joseph Cook, S. C. Willey, Moses C. Dole, Henry D. Wyatt, Gardiner Little, Jason Little, and Warren Tucker. Whole number of members from the organization of the Society to the present time, 200.

I will speak of some of the singing-schools and teachers. One taught by Sheldon Clark, the winter of 1817–1818, is spoken of as being a very popular school. Another, taught by Mr. Richardson, 1825–1826, as equally popular, and brought into the Society a large number of excellent singers. These two schools, I am told, were taught without the aid of any kind of musical instrument, thus raising up a class of independent singers, who could ever after stand alone, unsupported by an instrument. Mr. George taught the winter of 1835–1836. Rev. Worcester Willey, 1841–1842. This was an excellent school. I might also speak of Spencer, Blair, Wyatt, Adams, and Dearborn, as teachers who have subsequently taught, rendering acceptable service.

THE SABBATH SCHOOL.

BY CHARLES CUTTER.

THE Christian people of Campton were early interested in the biblical instruction of children. As long ago as 1812 or 1813, Mrs. Noyes, a widow lady residing on Pulsifer Hill, was accustomed to gather the children of her neighborhood together on the Sabbath to recite passages of Scripture, and to her seems to belong the honor of originating the first Sabbath School. Some ten or twelve years later a school was formed and held in an old barn that stood at the corner of the road near Mr. Farrar's, under the auspices of Mr. Jacob Giddings and Daniel Pulsifer. Here the children in the eastern part of the town, which then contained quite a large number of church-going people, were accustomed to stop for half an hour or more while on their way to meeting, and, seated upon planed boards, repeat passages from the Bible that they had committed to memory. Prayer and remarks from some one called upon to address them followed, and they then wended their way to the church. This school, not long after, was merged in one held at the church at noon, in which Dea. Willey, Dea. Bartlett, and several women were active in promoting its welfare. The session was held only in the summer season at this time, as there was no stove in the meeting-house, and it was necessary for the congregation to repair to the neighboring houses at noon in order to get warmed up for the afternoon service. The exercises of the school still continued to be recitation of Scripture, preceded by prayer, and closed by singing. In the year 1825 we have the record of the formation of a Sabbath School Society, whose object, as stated in the constitution adopted, was the establishment and instruction of a Sabbath School. Its officers were to consist of a president, secretary, librarian, and two super-intendents. Its members were to pay twenty cents yearly into the treas-ury. This Society, with some changes in its constitution, has continued down to the present time. From the period of its formation down to 1833, we have no record of its doings. The school meanwhile was kept up. A book entitled Biblical Catechism was used for a time, in which Scripture doctrines were stated, with proof texts thereof, which the scholars were expected to commit to memory. The year 1833 was the era of the advent of the Rev. Dr. Stone to the pastorate of the church. He appears to have infused new life into the Sabbath School. Through his influence nearly the whole congregation was induced to join the school in the study of the Bible, a feature which has been retained to this day, and is often adverted to by strangers called upon to address the school. The Union Question Books were introduced at about this time, and these were succeeded by various others down to the present year, when the Pilgrim Series of Uniform Lessons was adopted. In that year also a record of the doings of the Society began to be kept in a book; and, with the exception of the years 1836 and 1837, is entire down to the present time. Benjamin Noyes, Diadate Willey, Davis Baker, John Chandler, J. C. Blair, Moses C. Dole, Joseph Cook, are named in the record as having acted as superintendents. Up to 1845, in which year the article requiring a tax of twenty cents annually was struck from the constitution, the money received in this way, and by an occasional contribution, was ex-pended almost wholly upon the library. In the years 1833 and 1834, $33.95 were expended for this purpose. In 1835, 1836, and 1837, $34.67; in 1839, $13.45; in 1840, $10.63; in 1844, $6.50; in 1851, $20.61; in 1852, $16; in 1853, $6. In 1854, a monthly collection was voted, which has ever since been continued. In 1857, $12.33 were expended for the library; in 1859, $14.35 for that object, and $5 for mission schools; in 1860, $11.51 for books and papers; in 1861, $11.76 were expended for books and pa-pers, and $10 for tracts for the New Hampshire soldiers; in 1862, $2.05 for the latter object, $1.78 for books; in 1863, $10 for the soldiers and $15.72 for the library. 1864 marks the era of a great increase in the benevolent operations of the school. At the suggestion of Mr. Joseph Cook, the superintendent, several of the younger scholars went out soliciting funds for the establishment of a mission school. Their efforts resulted in the sum of $31.08, which was sent to the American Board, to be expended for that purpose; $26 also the same year were paid out for the library. In 1865 the young folks again went out, and collected $46.91. For various objects of benevolence this year the school paid out the sum of $144.48. In 1866, $20.05 were contributed for 200½ shares in the mission ship "Morning Star"; $26.10 were also expended for the library; $10 for the Congregational Society at Washington, D. C.; $20.84 for the Seaman's Friend Society at Boston.

In 1868 the Sabbath School Potato Fair was originated by the superintendent. The members of the school were invited to plant ten hills of potatoes each, the product to be disposed of at a Fair at the Town Hall in the fall, the money received to be devoted to a mission school. This institution has been kept up ever since. Not only potatoes but pumpkins, squashes, pop corn, etc., with various articles of female handiwork, have been brought in to increase the sale. A large number are usually present, and addresses and music add to the interest of the occasion. The proceeds of the Fair the first year amounted to $25.68. For the library and other purposes, that year, there were expended in all $103.37. In 1869 the Potato Fair resulted in the sum of $33. In 1870 the sale at the Potato Fair amounted to $32.75. A Christmas Festival was held this year, also, at Mr. J. C. Blair's, at which $8.10 were raised; there were expended for various objects, this year, $65.15. In 1871 the Potato Fair produced $42; the expenditure, the same year, reached the sum of $102.04. In 1872 the Potato Fair brought in $50; and in all $119.48 were expended. In 1873 $57 were realized from the Potato Fair; and $73.34 were devoted to various objects. Thus, in the last ten years, more than $800 have been raised and expended by the Sabbath School, and the amount of good it has accomplished can only be known to Him who knows the end from the beginning.

REMARKS OF REV. J. B. HADLEY.

Mr. President:

I think it not strange that the psalmist, in contemplating the material universe, was filled with rapturous thoughts in view of the exhibitions of the power, wisdom, and goodness of God, so strikingly displayed in the arrangement of the heavens and the earth to meet the necessary wants of the human family; not strange, that he, with a radiant countenance, should call upon the heavens, the earth, the seas, and everything that moveth therein, to praise the Lord, the Creator of all things.

Neither do I think it strange that the scientists of the present day, who believe in the atomical philosophy of the world's creation, see nothing in

the works of nature of divine power, wisdom, and goodness, to excite
lofty thoughts and to kindle in their souls a strong desire to love and
adore the Lord of all things. And what is this atomical theory? In brief
it is this: " That atoms and vacuum were the beginning of the universe;
these atoms were infinite in magnitude and number, and were borne
about through the universe in endless revolutions; and thus they produced
all the combinations that exist, — fire, water, air, earth; for all these are
only combinations of atoms, which are unchangeable. By the revolution
of these atoms the sun and moon were formed; the soul, the origin of
life, consciousness, and thought, was formed from the finest *fire atoms.*
Motion, then, is the cause of everything that exists."

If the fathers of this town had been believers in this theory, and had
brought up their children in the same faith, we should not have had a
centennial celebration here to-day. The names of the ten pastors, so
beautifully wreathed with evergreens upon these walls, whose labors God
blest to the salvation of many souls; the historical discourse replete with
stirring reminiscenses, the sweet tones of the organ blending harmoniously
with human voices, the large congregation now assembled in this house
of the Lord, all these cheerful sights and sounds, these soul-stirring incidents, would not have greeted our ears and cheered our eyes to-day.

Thanks to the Creator of the universe that such an atheistical senti-
ment did not dwarf the manhood and dry up the spiritual longings and
aspirations of those whose graves are with us, and whose holy living,
prayers and triumphant deaths are cherished with filial love.

And may it be the heartfelt prayer of all now present, that while the
silvery waters of our grand Pemigewasset flow onward, and while our
Palestine mountains shall stand firm upon their granite foundations, so
long may the glorious gospel be preached *here* to the honor of God and
to the salvation of coming generations.

REMARKS OF REV. N. BOUTON, D. D.

REV. DR. BOUTON, of Concord, said that he had listened with great interest to the historical discourse, and to the several papers which had been
read on this occasion, and hoped that all would be printed and thus be
preserved and handed down for future generations to read. The leading
idea which impressed his mind was the mission of a church, planted, like
this, in a rural district, small in numbers and weak in pecuniary re-
sources, yet sustaining itself with the ministry and ordinances of the
gospel through a hundred years. That mission, he said, was not merely
to conserve the peace and order of the surrounding community; to impart
religious instruction and send out moral and spiritual influences to the
people of a single town; not only to be a bond of fellowship and a means
of growth and usefulness to Christians, — but to raise up, from generation

to generation, a holy seed; to send out sons and daughters, well instructed, sanctified, and qualified to bless other portions of the country and of the world. In this regard, this church had nobly and well fulfilled its mission. Who can estimate the influences for good that have yearly flowed out like streamlets from the neighboring hills into all parts of our State and of our whole country? Count over the sons you have educated; follow them out to their several widely-extended spheres of labor, — furnishing deacons and pastors for city churches, and becoming themselves centres of wider and still wider circles of influence in remote sections of our country. Look, for illustration, to a single family planted on your hills. Accustomed to labor and privations in early life, struggling and pushing forward for higher and better advantages, three of them have become graduates of college; one of them, veteran pioneer and agent in every good work, has long been identified with the moral and religious interest of this State, has visited every town and neighborhood and hamlet, and left a Bible with prayers and counsels behind, to bless them. Another, teacher and editor, his good influence in younger life permeated an Eastern, and is now widely felt in a Western State. Another, a preacher and missionary among the Indians of the West, and a faithful laborer in other fields of service. And still another bears the honor, if not of *planting*, yet of being pastor of the first Congregational Church in California a number of years; of establishing and presiding over a college and State university; and is now pastor of a Congregational Church in Santa Cruz, Cal. If Campton had never done anything more than raise up and send out one such family, she had done a noble work, worthy of all praise. But your records show that this is not all; other illustrations might be given. I am surprised at the *persistence* with which good objects and good causes have been pursued. Your Sabbath School Organization, your Music Society, your Missionary Society, the annual amount of benevolent contributions, altogether, are a pattern for larger and more wealthy churches. My wish and prayer is that you may thus live and prosper through many generations.

REMARKS OF REV. WM. R. JEWETT.

MR. PRESIDENT:

It is many years since I have visited your town, but I am glad to be present on this interesting occasion. There is always a little of the melancholy in the feelings with which we revisit scenes that were once familiar, but have become strange by long absence. We live in a world of change. Everything around us is changing; we ourselves are constantly changing; yet ordinarily we take little notice of the changes that are silently taking place around us and within us.

But when, after an absence of many years, we return to a place where once we were familiar, the changes of the past rush upon the mind, and the pleasure we enjoy is mingled with sadness. Nearly thirty years ago, on an exchange with the clergyman who was then your pastor, I visited this town for the first time. The people assembled for worship, not in this sanctuary, but in the old-fashioned meeting-house on a neighboring hill, which many of you will remember, with its numerous ranges of square pews below, its galleries with its ranges of wall-pews.

The people of Campton went up to the temple to worship. At that time there was a class of hearers in this congregation (and I hope the class has not become extinct) who lived upon the strong meat of scriptural truth, and who by use had "their senses exercised to discern both good and evil." Nothing but such food was relished.

When I received the polite invitation of your committee to be present to-day, at once my purpose was taken to revisit the romantic town, with its beautiful hills and its mountain gorges, its shady groves and its lovely valleys, watered by that river which contributes so much to the fertility and beauty of this whole region.

Still more, I wished to revive ancient associations connected with a hundred localities in this vicinity, — to meet and to greet my old friends, and to be greeted by them as only friends are greeted who return after a long absence.

Many that I once knew and loved are gone from the place, — many are dead. The graves of some of my old friends and parishioners are found in your cemetery. Now that I have changed my home my thoughts often go back to Beech Hill and Prospect Hill.

I have lived in cordial friendship with all your pastors for thirty years. The late Dr. Stone had resigned the pastoral charge of the church and was Secretary of the New Hampshire Missionary Society when I entered my new field of labor. With him I quickly formed acquaintance which ripened into the most hearty friendship, and continued unbroken to the hour of his death. Allow me to pay a short tribute to his memory. He was not distinguished for creative imagination, or possessed great power over the passions or sensibilities of his hearers. His mind was of a strictly logical cast. In soundness of judgment he excelled almost any man with whom I have ever had acquaintance. Hence his great influence with the trustees of the Missionary Society. They had learned from long experience that he was a safe and judicious counsellor. The reports of the Missionary Society, that he prepared for twenty years, were listened to with the deepest interest. They were reports such as few secretaries have prepared, or could prepare.

With the Rev. Charles Shedd, who became your pastor in 1842, my acquaintance was of the most intimate character. How often have I heard a rap at the door of my study, and upon rising to open, have found Brother Shedd standing at the entrance. I can truly say of this good man what President Edwards says of himself: " He loved the doctrines of the gospel; they were to his soul like green pastures. The doctrines of God's absolute sovereignty and free grace in showing mercy to whom he would show mercy, and man's absolute dependence on the operations of God's Holy Spirit, appeared to him as sweet and glorious doctrines."

These doctrines were his delight. Once on an exchange I met him half-way between our habitations. He commenced at once by saying, " Brother Jewett, my mind of late has been greatly exercised on the doctrine of election. It is a glorious doctrine. It exalts God and it humbles man." On the evening of the same day, in returning, we met again; he then said, " Brother Jewett, my mind has of late been greatly absorbed in contemplating the doctrine of divine sovereignty. It is a glorious doctrine." It is possible that at some periods in his ministry he gave too much prominence to his favorite themes, however true and important, and left a wrong impression on the minds of his hearers. I was greatly interested in hearing the letter which was read from him to-day. He is still in his Western home, preaching the gospel which he so much loved, and bringing forth fruit in his old age. May the blessing of God be with him always!

Of his worthy successor I need say nothing, for he is present and has spoken for himself.

My Brethren and Friends, — The remaining moments of this occasion are fast approaching their close. We thank God that we have been permitted to engage in these services on this beautiful day, and under this smiling sun, and to listen to the instructive and valuable discourse of your present pastor, in whom you are so happily united. We now part, to be scattered far and wide, but often as we remember this occasion, often as we look back to these hills and valleys, we shall exclaim as the Hebrew prophet did of Jerusalem, "If I forget thee let my right hand forget her cunning; if I do not remember thee let my tongue cleave to the roof of my mouth.'

Here we have no continuing city, but there is a city which has foundations, whose builder and maker is God. Its foundations are garnished with all manner of precious stones, and each gate is a pearl. May we at last, through the riches of grace, be accepted as citizens of the heavenly Jerusalem, and join in the worship of the upper world, entering upon an everlasting progress of holiness and bliss !

REMARKS OF REV. ISAAC WILLEY.

IN the preservation of this church through the century of its existence the hand of God is as clearly manifest as in any period in the history of his ancient church. The town itself among the hills and necessarily small, nearly surrounded by towns in which the institutions of religion were not statedly maintained; a large portion of its people on the west side of the river worshipping at Plymouth; another part sustaining a Baptist Church; many of its valuable farms in the hands of those who

6

felt no interest in the church, — is it not marvellous that this church has lived and prospered as it has? Here the public worship of God has continued without interruption one hundred years. Often the number of families co-operating in its support has been less than forty, and many of these securing from these hills but a small income from their labor. For a very large portion of the time the ministry has been sustained here, and always without aid from any foreign source. A fact of interest is that the early population of this town were brought up to support religious institutions and to attend upon public worship on the Sabbath. Many of these persons were not members of the church, but they stood by it and made sacrifices for its support.

Another fact of interest is the well-known liberality of this church to the benevolent objects of the day. It has frequently occurred that the amount of their contributions equalled the salary of their minister. This accounts, in no small measure, for its stability and its prosperity. They trusted in the Lord and did good, "so they have dwelt in the land, and verily, they have been fed." Of the men who officiated in the ministry here we have already heard. My recollection extends back three fourths of the century. I have a distinct recollection of all the ministers except the first, and of him I have ever entertained a high regard from the impressions received from my parents and others. Rev. Mr. Chapin was a tall, spare man, of consistent and sober deportment. Mother wit, of which he had his share, would only occasionally appear. He refused to be settled according to ecclesiastical usage, saying that he was like his horse, sure to break away if tied. He was a Congregationalist in his views of church polity. Of the Church of England he said that at the Reformation they swept the dirt into the porch and left it there. He was a benevolent man. An instance is recollected of his meeting a poor boy, on a frosty morning, and of his taking off his coat and putting it upon him. He was opposed to instrumental music; and the bass-viol was laid aside. " What would you say," said he, " if I should place a wooden minister in the pulpit? You do no better, in introducing a wooden singer." A regard to his feelings, rather than his argument, influenced the people at the time. He became interested in politics; gave a warm support to the election of Mr. Jefferson as President. He embraced the views of the Baptist denomination, and declined any longer serving this church. He preached elsewhere as he was invited, and attended many funerals. In his advanced years, he became destitute of the means of a comfortable living. He was once called upon for a tax of half a dollar; he replied that he had not received as much for his services for many years. Of his family, made up of his wife and daughter, I cannot forbear saying a word. Intelligent, discreet, devoted Christians, their influence was felt for good by all who knew them.

Mr. Webber was a man of commanding personal influence. His preaching was often impressive and instructive. But his large family and small salary made it necessary for him to labor for their support. His services on the Sabbath were consequently not as well matured as they otherwise might have been, but he was useful in his day. His labors immediately preceded the great revival of 1815. Of him the following incident is remembered: In his rides through the parish he one day fell in with Col. C., a young man of popular talents, but not of fixed religious principles, and he remarked to him that he only occasionally saw him at church. The colonel replied that he frequently attended other meetings. "Is it not wise," said Mr. Webber, "to have a stated place of meeting?" "Oh!" said the colonel, "it is said that a change of pastures makes fat calves." Said Mr. Webber, "I once knew a case where a calf sucked two cows all the season."—"And what did he make?" said the colonel. "A *great calf!*" was the reply.

During the great revival and the year following a number of men labored here in the ministry for a time, as we have learned from Mr. Blakely. But soon came the question as to the settlement of a minister. The Society was then confined, mainly, to the east side of the river, and they knew not how to raise the means for his support. At this time, Mr. Brown, from Thornton, had been making some preparation for preaching, under the care of Rev. Dr. Wood, of Boscawen. He was induced to enter upon the work here, upon a small salary. He was an earnest Christian man, and after the labors of a few years removed to the West.

At the settlement of Rev. Mr. Hale, both parts of the town united, and worship was sustained a portion of the time on each side of the river. His ministry was connected not only with the enlargement of the church, but with the increase of the means for the support of its institutions. He sought the interests of this people by much personal sacrifice; and so far as we can now see, might have remained here with comfort to himself and with benefit to the people the few years which he was permitted to live. Here he buried his companion. He removed to Maine, where, after a few years, he married again. At his death, his widow assumed the responsibility of caring for and educating his children; and most faithfully did she perform these duties. The two sons, in early manhood, were ripened for and departed to the rest of the people of God. The daughter still lives, and is the wife of Rev. Lauren Armsby, Council Cove, Kan.

Mr. Willey gave pleasing reminiscences, and bore honorable testimony to the character of several of the early deacons of the church. Deacon Wyatt's—"the honest miller"—character was formed after the model of Dr. Watts, whose sermons he read and whose hymns he sung. Deacon Burbeck was an exemplary and thoughtful man, of humble pretensions. He read much, and his more worldly neighbors regarded him as sometimes neglecting his worldly interests; but another day may show that in seeking first the Kingdom of Heaven and its righteousness, he pursued the wiser course. Deacon Bartlett had his early training under the ministry of Dr. Spring, of Newburyport, which prepared him for the service to which he was frequently called. There being no vestry, meetings for prayer and for other purposes were numerous at his house. Few families but would have esteemed this a burden; but the blessing of the house of Obed-Edom has been upon that family.

After the establishment of the Theological Seminary at Andover by the munificence of his brother, the late William Bartlett, of Newburyport, and Dr. Griffin had been appointed professor, Deacon Bartlett was so anxious to hear him preach that he made a journey to Andover for that purpose. It is not too much to say that all he had anticipated was fully realized. Another incident: two young men, preparing for the ministry, came to Deacon Bartlett's house one Sabbath noon, from an excursion among the mountains. They were not of the most sober kind. Themselves and team were well cared for. But they did not leave the next morning without such a reproof for their levity and their violation of the Sabbath as they never afterwards forgot. They both became distinguished ministers in Massachusetts, but were never the worse for the lesson which they received from Deacon Bartlett.

Deacon Diadate Willey spoke with much feeling of his interest in the occasion. His own memory went back over three fourths of the period we now review. He was a subject of the great revival in 1815. He seemed burdened with the desire that this people might now enjoy a like refreshing from on high. He earnestly exhorted all to accept the gracious provisions of the gospel for our salvation.

David Bartlett, another subject of the revival of 1815, gave interesting reminiscences of his uncle, Ebenezer Bartlett, Jr. He spoke of the good influence of a certain sermon by Rev. Mr. Hovey, from the text, " Who is on the Lord's side?" Also of another, by Rev. Mr. Day, from the text, " The harvest is past, the summer is ended, and we are not saved." He said that twenty were struck under conviction while listening to that sermon.

SKETCHES OF PIETY.

FURNISHED BY REV. AND MRS. AUSTIN WILLEY.

It will certainly be gratifying to the church to note down such recollections of Deacon Ebenezer Bartlett as Mrs. Willey, his only remaining child, and myself, may have, although he was a member of the church in Plymouth after 1800 in consequence of his residence.

He was a citizen of the town, and nearly all his other connections were there. Most of his children and relatives were in the church in Campton, and he ever cherished a deep interest in its welfare. His prayers may have secured for it many blessings, and in the roll of pious memories there, we cannot leave him out. He, with his brother David, were early emigrants, and brought with them from Newburyport, Mass., decided Christian characters. He came when seventeen years of age. He had a strong desire to prepare for the ministry, but his father was unwilling. It was a sad mistake; his life was half minister as it was. He had a strong desire for knowledge and culture, and improved every means within his reach in a new country. His taste was refined, and his love for solid reading was strong. He early obtained a share in that old library and enriched his mind by its stores. When a young man, he, his brother, and a relative ("Corporal Bartlett"), working together among the logs, by agreement corrected and aided each other in the best use of language,—a rare thing for pioneer emigrants,—and they all, especially the brothers, acquired a propriety of language which greatly increased their usefulness. In his later years, he wrote some, and well, for publication. Mrs. Willey says, "My earliest impressions of my father are that he was a very holy man, and lived nearer to heaven than any other person I ever knew. There seemed about him a kind of halo, which, as a child, I thought resembled heaven; but such was his sweetness, his gentleness and affection, that we were not overawed by his sacredness. We revered, but loved him not the less. I never heard him speak an improper word. Family worship morning and night was faithfully observed, and he often added a few words to the reading. His prayers were far from formal; they were tender, earnest, and particular, especially for the children, that "God would remember his covenant to all generations," and that "each one might be prepared to die."

He was not lengthy, but enough so to make the service always impressive. The children never forgot that family worship. So strong were his impressions of life's uncertainty, he many times made this service as though it might be the last. My father was strict in reference to the Sabbath. It was a holy day. All chores and labor were done, when possible, before sunset Saturday night, and the evening was spent in reading and religious conversation, preparatory to the Sabbath. It was his desire that as little work as possible should be done in the house and out of it. He disallowed all unnecessary secular conversation and reading, and the children's play must go over till Monday. We had a regular exercise every Sabbath, all the children repeating the Commandments and Catechism, and listening to his pious conversation. We used, also, to sing. He loved religious worship, and although four miles from meeting, he was very seldom absent, nor was most of the family,—and it was before the days of carriages. His attendance on other religious meetings was equally exact. I have known him, when at work in the field, and the family could not attend the monthly concert, to put up his team, come to the house, call the family together, read from the Bible, talk upon it, and offer earnest prayer. One time, I remember, he read the 11th of Hebrews,—a great favorite of his,—and his heart was so full that he poured out his soul in prayer and tears. He dwelt upon the examples of faith in that great army of patriarchs and heroes till he seemed to stand among them. After returning on the Sabbath, with its two services, he generally held a meeting on Beech Hill, in the evening, and closed the day in devout family and private worship. Such were our old Sabbaths, begun by him an hour earlier than his usual rising for devotional purposes.

He maintained a kind but firm authority in the family as a scriptural duty and his children revered while they loved him. Age had no acidity for him. Like the patriarch Joseph, children's children climbed upon his knees with mutual fondness. He enjoyed pleasantry, if polished and sensible, and social life ever found him congenial. His humility was prominent in his character. Its opposites were especially odious. A friend at table one day began repeating a remark respecting his usefulness in the church, when he quickly beckoned to him to stop. And this quality of character he sought to cultivate in his children.

Of his own religious experience he said little. With such a life it was scarcely necessary. It spoke for itself. His views of God's perfections were so exalted and glorious that his "joy" was sometimes too "full" for suppression. One day he was plowing, and the passage came to him with great power, " Break up your fallow ground." Such a view of the sinfulness of his own heart was opened to him as to overwhelm him and oblige him to leave his team and pour out his soul before God in strong crying and tears, where he found relief. At another time when he was laying stone wall, the words, " The stone which the builders rejected," brought to him such a view of Christ as to be unutterable and full of glory. He knew what the Saviour meant when saying, " I will manifest myself to him "; " he walked with God."

I never knew him leave home for a journey in the middle of the day without calling his family together for prayer. I never knew him repeat an injurious report of any one, and he so instructed his children. His practice was to go first to the accused. When we had company, the occasion was usually closed with prayer. He seldom went where young people were without speaking to them about the salvation of their souls. And often when passing them in the road he would do the same.

He had ten children. One died in infancy, and one at sixteen years of age. The others all lived to be heads of families, — one excepted, — and all united with Congregational churches, six with the church in Campton and two elsewhere. That all his children, as he hoped, had given their hearts to the Saviour, was regarded by him as the dearest blessing of a covenant-keeping God.

His integrity and profound regard for justice are seen in an incident. He was chosen as a referee in a case between two neighbors. After hearing all the evidence, the other referees at once gave their decision; but although the case was plain, he must wait till another day, for he might be wrong, and wished time for reflection, and no doubt for prayer. No one, it is presumed, ever complained of him for not fulfilling every promise which he made. With him it was religion.

The eminent piety of Mr. Bartlett was nowhere more apparent than as a member and officer of the church. He was a pillar. Religion was very low in Plymouth for many years; its vitality seemed to flicker faintly in all but a few hearts. Rev. Jno. Ward preached the gospel faithfully, but he had very little co-operation, and death reigned. In all these long, dark years Deacon Bartlett stood by him as a brother in sympathy and in labor. He was never of robust health, and in his later years he could not bear hard, constant labor. His voice also failed, so that for many years he could speak only in whisper; but his articulation was so distinct that he could be heard. The prayer-meeting rarely found him absent, or itself without vitality when he was there. And he spent much time in visiting from house to house, urging immediate attention to the soul's salvation, and praying with the families. After long years of "sowing in tears," the harvest came. The town was shaken to the bottom, a large number were converted, and he was permitted to see the church and Society generally enter upon a new life. His labors, with those of his beloved pastor, had been abundantly blessed, even beyond their faith. His own spiritual life rose still higher, and

" Bright rays of setting lustre
Shone on his evening hours."

His final sickness was brief and tranquil. He could say little, and little remained to be said. He quieted the solicitude of his family by assuring them of God's constant care. But he distinctly expressed his triumphant faith by repeating the whole passage, " I am persuaded that neither death nor life, nor angels, nor principalities, nor powers, nor things present, nor things to come, nor height, nor depth, nor any other creature, shall be able to separate us from the love of God which is in Christ Jesus our Lord." And so he entered into the joy of his Lord. It was not death. He only slept — rested. No death-scenes were there. He never looked more lovely than in the coffin. The beauty of holiness adorned it, and fragrance from the upper Eden embalmed the precious form. Such a death, so " precious in the sight of the Lord," could only be sweetly glorious to Christian affection. The funeral theme by Rev. Mr. Punchard was, " My father, my father! the chariot of Israel and the horsemen thereof." He, with our faithful mother, rest together in your cemetery till the mortal puts on the immortal.

But to his precious memory we offer this tribute of affection, and venture to present to that old beloved church this example of Christian character gathered from the first half of the first century to inspire and to enrich the second. Those valleys and hills were baptized in their infancy by the Holy Spirit, and the consecration has been repeated again and again down the ages of its history. The fathers and mothers, though dead, yet speak, and in example live. Their monuments testify to the grace of God in Jesus Christ, and to the inheritance they secured by covenant for "thousands of generations" "to such as keep his commandments to do them."

OTHER SKETCHES.

The later Scriptures dwell with great delight upon the grace of God in the piety of preceding ages. Well indeed if the inspired example were better followed, "telling it to children's children, that they may put their hope in God." The Holy Spirit has dwelt in these beautiful valleys and on these hillsides from the first settlement of the town. There was Miss Sally Chapin, only child of Rev. Mr. Chapin, pastor of the church. She was a cripple, but taught school every summer, and was my first teacher. She was humble and devoted, and her faithful labors and prayers for her scholars left impressions which no time can efface. She read the Bible, talked so earnestly and lovingly to us, and prayed so tenderly and devoutly, that impressions were made which are verdant still. Many little children, as well as older scholars, were led by her to Christ and his service. I have never seen a better example of usefulness by a devoted young woman in school. That was seventy years ago, and "her works do follow her" still. I know of eight who were impressed first by her efforts, and have lived Christian lives.

Another intelligent, praying woman was Mrs. Fletcher, sister of the late Major Pulsifer. She was a model of good sense and of devout piety, and many received great assistance from her prayers and counsels, especially during the great revival. She had a large family of children, and all were saved, it is believed, by her endeavors. So sure is God's covenant.

There was Miss Betsey Palmer, a humble, praying woman, fifty-five years ago. I remember well how constant she was in the choir, singing so devoutly her counter with feeble voice. The Saviour was with her.

Miss Pearsons, a young lady from Haverhill, N. H., resided some time in Campton, and taught our school. She brought the Holy Spirit with her. All loved her, especially her scholars, many of whom were led to the Saviour by her gentle hand. I well remember how her pale lips trembled in anxious prayer for her scholars, while she knelt in school. She died not long after; but the sheaves from her sowing are not all gathered yet.

Dr. Morrison, "the beloved physician," settled here soon after the great revival, and from a similar one in Hanover. He was eminently useful in elevating the Christian character, especially the young people. He was a good singer, and did much to impart to it culture and devotion. That old Music Society owes much of its origin to him. But death soon gave him a part in the "new song," and many a tear has been shed upon his grave.

There was Deacon David Bartlett, who stood as a central pillar in that church for half the century you review. He stood firmly when darkness and difficulties hung over it. When its pastor forsook its faith and led away all he could, he, with Deacon Burbeck, Deacon Wyatt, and a few others, held the ark steadily and carried it forward. They were able men in the Scriptures, — better theologians than are always found in the pulpit. They were men of thought and intelligence, and more than all, men of prayer and steady, active piety. For many years they had no minister, and these men sustained the regular worship with ability and spiritual effect. Meetings were about as large as when there was a minister. A sermon was read by some good reader, — Jacob Gidding was the best, — a sermon by one of the old masters, instructive, pungent, and powerful, very different from popular pulpit essays of the present. I remember, when a child, the prayers of these men, and others who took part with them. They were solemn and earnest for men who were "lost" — "dead" — and must be aroused and saved quickly, or die forever. And their hymns had the same tone. Deacon Burbeck's favorite was, "And are we wretches yet alive?" How often he read that! So, also, "Is this the kind return." They were not perfect, but their stable, consistent lives gave influence to the religion they maintained. Such were some of the men and women who gave vitality and strength to that church in the past; to whose prayers the Holy Ghost witnessed wondrously, and by whom it has been handed down to you, baptized for another century. Their graves will be increasingly precious, and "their memorial shall endure throughout all generations." Who are to be their successors in the opening century? If, as in the past, that is to be a missionary church still, may it gladly accept the honor; increase and train its missionary emigrants for Christ's service, and never forget them in your prayers, nor let them forget you. Allow me affectionately to suggest this as one measure to begin with : Not satisfied with the past, embrace the entire town not elsewhere connected, old and young; visit every family and person, to save and enlist them for Christ, allowing no doubt but God's Spirit will go with you.

LETTER FROM REV. AND MRS. AUSTIN WILLEY.

NORTHFIELD, MINN., Sept. 18, 1874.

TO THE COMMITTEE OF THE CONGREGATIONAL CHURCH IN CAMPTON:

Dear Brethren, — Your card of invitation to attend your centennial is received, awakening a throng of old recollections and affections, as of a mother. Most gladly would we share personally with you the rich occasion before you, but that privilege we cannot have. But we will still be there, in sympathy, in affection, in thanksgiving and confession, in prayer, and renewed consecration and hope. We will again mingle in your songs of praise and supplication; and we ask you to include us in the footing-up of "the children which God has given you" in the century you review. And let us contribute to the recollections of piety which you will bring to remembrance the sketch of our devoted parent, which

7

we send you. May the grace of God be more richly yours in the future than in the past, and enable that church to show at the end of the century a still higher record of its usefulness than in the past. All things are ready; and we ask that you, as a church, do not forget your children, however scattered, while we will never forget you.

Yours in Christian affection,
A. WILLEY.
JUDITH B. WILLEY.

Rev. Q. Blakely and others.

LETTER FROM SYLVESTER MARSH.

Littleton, Oct. 19, 1874.

Rev. Quincy Blakely and others of Centennial Committee :

Gentlemen, — I had intended being with you to-morrow, but unforeseen circumstances will prevent. It will be an occasion of great interest, in which I should participate with all my heart. Let us remember that the fathers who established the church are in the midst of realities upon which we shall have entered long before another centennial shall roll around.

Yours in faith and hope,
SYLVESTER MARSH.

LETTER FROM REV. G. I. BARD, OF MEREDITH VILLAGE, N. H.

East Boston, 17 October, 1874.

C. M. Bartlett :

Dear Brother, — I regret very much that sickness and the need of recruiting have taken me so far away at the time of your centennial celebration. It would give me great pleasure to be with you and participate in exercises commemorative of the birth of a church older than the government under which we live, — a church which has been permitted to live and prosper and work during the lapse of a century full of such great events. In our earlier history the Congregational Church in New England was called the "*Standing Order.*" I exult in the record of *standing* during all these years. In a work entitled, "First Century of National Existence," I find it asserted that our order, during the last quarter of a century, has risen up to new life, and that during the war of the Rebellion it showed itself efficient in its work in the great West. I feel confident of the truth that the very existence of our government to-day is due largely to the vigor of our order in the States of the great West and Northwest. I find that in our very earliest history a few churches were planted in the South. We have a great work to do in that region. Let it be understood that Congregational churches for the South is the best reconstruction of the South. If anything means liberty it is

Congregationalis..1. We have much to do in the century to come. Let us hold ourselves open to all light, and forward and foremost in all progress. Max Muller says, "A religion that does not *grow* is *dead.*" But we shall never outgrow Jesus Christ, our head, and those great truths which you have been sustaining: only let us keep in line with all the progress of events; let us advance to all the duties of the hour. I have lived long enough near by you to know the great worth and influence of your church under its past and present leadership. I join my prayers and praises with you on your anniversary day. With great regret, I cannot be with you,

I am yours in brotherly love,

G. L BARD.

LETTER FROM REV. DANIEL PULSIFER.

DANBURY, July 16, 1874.

DEACON BROWN:

Dear Sir, — Yours of the 6th inst. has been received, and I feel pleased that the church in Campton think to celebrate the one hundredth anniversary of its existence. I do hope that it will prove a good season; that the Holy Spirit will be shed down upon you like "rain upon the mown grass"; and that the time for another similar meeting will not arrive ere the voice of a great multitude shall be heard "saying, Alleluia! for the Lord God Omnipotent reigneth." It is not very probable that I shall be able to attend the meeting, though I should like to very much; for the state of my health is such that it is quite uncertain whether I ever visit Campton again. . . . Please tender my Christian affection to the members of the church, especially to the older ones, with whom I used to be acquainted, and ask them to remember me in their prayers, infirm and unworthy as I am, that by the grace of God I may be fitted to enjoy God's love in heaven; and there, with all the redeemed from among men, to celebrate His praise forever and ever. Oh, for Christ's sake, may God grant it to us all. . . . I would say to all the members of the church that it is the prayer of your unworthy brother, "The grace of our Lord Jesus Christ be with you all."

Yours affectionately,

DANIEL PULSIFER.

LETTER FROM MRS. BENJ. P. STONE, RYE BEACH.

THE memories of that dear old parsonage at Campton come to me like the pleasant sunset glintings upon these rugged rocks of the sea-shore, where I am now resting. A thousand delightful incidents loom up in tender beauty through the haze of those far-gone years. If ever there was a God-honored parish, Campton was it. Men of bone and sinew were its founders; and the love of truth, eternal truth, planted their homesteads. There the sons and daughters grew up a God-fearing race, and peace and competence were their portion. No one who ever took his stand at the door of the old church, forty years ago, could doubt their love of the worship of the sanctuary. Whole double wagon-loads of people drove up, and with such glad, cheery faces as told you, " This is our Holy Day." Little children, in no small number, were of the assembly; for all those men of God and those mothers in Israel believed that " Instead of thy fathers shall be thy children," and they trained those children to come forward to the work.

This it is which has kept Campton church from becoming feeble. The spirit of self-denial has been drawn in with mother's milk; and thus, while many another church of quite as much wealth has called for assistance, they have nobly borne their own burdens.

Few parishes have cared better for their pastors. What they promised they promptly paid; and then, besides, they never forgot their minister's family, when, from time to time, any special rarity came to their sharing. One of the pleasant fruits of this early and continued Christian living is seen in the fact that the old homesteads are not forsaken to the extent so sadly realized in most of our rural towns. Good, strong, earnest young men are found there, ready to put their shoulder to the wheel, and looking not so much for earthly gains as to the approval of conscience and to the fulfilment of the work assigned them, knowing that in the infinite future it shall come about in many a case that " the last shall be first and the first last."

LETTER FROM REV. CHARLES SHEDD.

WASECA, MINN., Sept. 8, 1874.

To THE CHURCH OF CHRIST IN CAMPTON, N. H.:

Brethren Beloved, — It would give me great pleasure to be with you in person, according to your invitation, and take part with you in your centennial celebration. I regret that I cannot do so. I find the infirmities of age growing upon me, and deterring me from undertaking so long a journey. I shall, if my life is spared to the 20th proximo, see the last day of my seventy-second year. Then it will be very suitable for me to be with you in spirit, and with you to review the past. Trusting that the occasion will be one of great spiritual benefit to you, I present to you, through this letter, my cordial salutations, congratulations, and good wishes. The history of your church for the one hundred years past is the essential history of your place. The history of the church of Christ at large, including all its various influences, is the history of all that is good and valuable in the world. The Bible contains the history of redemption and not much else. There is nothing worth recording which does not grow out of the kingdom of heaven on earth, or that is not intimately associated with the work of reforming and saving a lost world. The last century is full of great events, all of such a nature as to convince the most sceptical that the kingdom is coming. I have nothing to say against other church organizations. They are doing their great and good work. They differ somewhat from ours. They originated under monarchy, and still partake of the characteristics of monarchy. Congregationalism draws both its outward and inward life from the inspired volume, recognizes liberty, equality, and fraternity as essential attributes in church and state, was constructed on the Mayflower, lived and acted in the New England churches, and gave birth to the system of free government under which we live. The leaven of the Plymouth colony was infused into the increasing population of the surrounding region, setting up the school-house as well as the meeting-house, for the maintenance of its great principles of equality and freedom, until the opposition of monarchy was brought to bear in the struggle of the Revolution. The resistance on our part to the oppression of the mother-country was the result of the moral power of the Congregational churches. That great Revolution, giving rise to so many other similar ones in different parts of the world, occurred at the commencement of the century which you now review. Your own Christian fathers saw that sanguinary event and took part in it. Then the opposition of monarchy being overcome, the republican bud blossoms out into the general government; the little germ becomes a tree, which expands itself over a wide domain, under whose branches the nation hoped to rest in peace. But there was a worm at the root which marred the beauty of the tree and threatened its entire destruction. That worm was slavery, and Slavery began the conflict. Then in the North, Freedom arose in her might to assert and maintain her rights. Freedom prevails and Slavery dies, but with it many of our dear ones who had else been here to-day, fell a sacrifice. My first-born found a grave in southern soil. Many of your sons, likewise, some of whom I accounted my children in the gospel, shared a similar fate. Do you wonder that I can sympathize with you to-day during this rehearsal of our common experience? But we are alike comforted with the thought that the leaven of righteousness, under Providence, was working off the scum of ungodliness in the nation. It was the result of the operation of that truth of which the church is the pillar and ground. But freedom, though associated with the very existence of our church organization, is not confined to our own land. It passes over the seas. The nations are in commotion; they behold the wonders wrought here, and they ask for similar forms of government and privileges with us. All these things have taken place within the limits of this century, and yet much more. There are currents in the ocean, which though less conspicuous than the rolling of the waves and the ebbing and flowing of the tides, are not less beneficial and useful. I refer to the great reformatory, humanizing, and saving efforts which have had their origin in our churches during the last half or three quarters of the century, and which diffuse the gospel life and spirit of our churches to the utmost bounds. I need hardly name the Bible Society, the Missionary Societies, foreign and domestic; the

Seamen's cause, the Tract, Temperance, Education, and Sabbath School causes, with others too numerous to mention. These are working more than literal miracles. Christ recognizes the spiritual works of his people as greater than his own literal ones. These causes are dear to you. They have called for your aid, and you have always responded.

Again, I will just refer to those revival scenes which have occurred within the recollection of some now present; those new creations, those resurrections from death in sin to newness of life, which brought salvation to yourselves and others, waked up the joys of heaven on earth, and glorified the King of kings. You prayed for them; you labored for them; you rejoiced in them; you were edified by them; you can never forget them; they will pass in review to-day, as the spiritual birthdays of the fathers and the children, and the glory of your Zion. But the limits of a letter must limit the flow of my thoughts and feelings. This is a solemn occasion. This day closes the century of your church's being and history. Old in years, as we reckon human life, but yet, as we trust, only in the beginning of its vigor and usefulness, may she live on without growing old, till all the centuries of the world shall have passed, and till her last members shall be changed in a moment, in the twinkling of an eye. But the fathers who founded this church and nourished it in its weakness, so as always to render it independent of foreign charity, — where now are those worthies? How gladly we would hail them here on this occasion! Their immediate successors, too. They rest from their labors, and their works do follow them; and ye are witnesses that they did not labor in vain. Their very names are precious; you will delight to call them to-day, though they cannot answer.

Brethren and friends, may you profit by this occasion. God willing, you will enter to-morrow on the duties and responsibilities of a new century. The past is full of wonders. The next, we doubt not, will tell more than before of the progress of the kingdom. Begin it with prayer to the great Head of the church, and humble consecration to the work before you. Then will the Lord God dwell in the midst of you, and make your peace as a river and your righteousness as the waves of the sea. In a few more years, we who are alive shall meet, pastor and people, on a greater occasion than this, and joyfully rehearse all the good way in which the Lord hath led his people. Will all this assembly be there? And will there be no disappointments on that occasion?

Yours, in the fellowship of the Gospel,
CHARLES SHEDD.

LETTER FROM REV. S. H. WILLEY, D. D.

FIRST CONGREGATIONAL CHURCH, SANTA CRUZ, CAL., Oct. 10, 1874.

REV. QUINCY BLAKELY:

Dear Brother, — It gives me pleasure to acknowledge the receipt of the invitation to be present and participate in the celebration of the one hundredth anniversary of the church in Campton, on the 20th inst.

My home is so far away from the old New Hampshire hills that it will be impossible for me to be there, but I shall be deeply interested in the proceedings. I could not contribute much to the interest of the occasion if I were there, nor can I do it by letter; but there are members of my family who can, and I hope some of them will be with you.

I left Campton when a boy of only fourteen years of age. Of course, I know the town and the church only as a boy. But the church was a good mother to me. The first minister I remember was Rev. Mr. Hale. I was a little afraid of him when he was not in the pulpit, but when he was there, where I was used to seeing him, I listened to a great deal he said. There were some "protracted meetings" in 1831, I think, and a good many of us young folks became personally interested in religion. We gave up our nonsense on Sunday noons, and went regularly out under the pines on the river bank, and held social religious meetings. Those meetings were honest and sincere, certainly on the part of many, and did much to forecast a Christian life that followed. I think I could cross the continent and go to the spot where that prayer-meeting used to be held, now. But very few who used to attend it could be assembled in this world. But some have been good men and good women, and have finished their course with joy, — some in the ministry and some in the mission field.

Pretty soon Mr. Hale left; we boys did not know why, and for that matter, I don't know why to this day. But he went away, and we young folks were in a fair way of becoming wanderers, when Rev. B. P. Stone became our pastor.

I don't think he was a very young man, but he had a young wife, bright, cheery, enterprising; skilful in enlisting the interest of "young gentlemen and ladies" in their teens, and setting them inquiring what they were made for and what was the best thing they could do with themselves. So, while her husband studied and preached, she talked, and drew us out, set us to reading and directed and even provided that reading; and I remember what a new and wonderful world this seemed to me to be. Somebody came along preaching about Oberlin and the "far West," and what great issues were to be determined there, and how they wanted teachers and preachers. An intelligent, Christian interest grew among us. Working on the farm or going to school, I wondered what part I could take in this great kingdom.

The first step plainly was to profess Christ. That step was taken reverently and sincerely, and under thorough instruction from the pastor. For myself it was the welcome to the church and at the same time the parting, for I went at once away to the academy to fit for college. But the spirit of the church, as I remember it, was the spirit of earnest Christian devotion and Christian service. The tone of those years was an earnest tone. There was breadth to the plans and ideas that I remember hearing talked about. Folks in that little mountain town of a little over a thousand inhabitants were planning and giving and praying for the great country towards the setting sun and for the missions in foreign lands. And we children grew up with the idea that our lives had something material to do with the salvation of the country and the world, And now, when the noble old church comes to complete her first century, I feel like coming with those, her children, who assemble to bring her a crumb of honor. Through her nurture, including in it that of home, public worship, Sunday School, prayer-meeting, and missionary concerts, we come to have our first ideas of life, its worth and its duties. For one I can testify that these ideas have been ever present and controlling. Just as I completed my studies and entered the ministry, the acquisition of California made it necessary that some one should follow the flag here in the service of the gospel.

It was a remote and then unknown region, with not a school-house or a Protestant church or a Protestant minister known to be in it. But people were beginning to come, now that it was United States territory, though the news of the gold discovery had not got across the continent yet. Under the motives then presented, it was the natural consequence of the church instructions and influence of my childhood that I should come. It was merely following the motives in early manhood, that I had felt the full force of, time and again, in the old church in Campton in childhood. And now I am reminded just to say that this very year we are celebrating here the twenty-fifth anniversary of the beginnings of our Christian work of which I have spoken. We number some five hundred Protestant churches, and rejoice in an excellent system of public education, exceedingly well provided and amply sustained. People came for gold and silver, and they got a good deal of both; but they *stay* because they find it a great wheat-growing, wool-producing, grazing, and commercial country, with almost every variety of healthful climate in which to live.

So the good old mother church in Campton may have her share of joy in her one hundredth year in the celebrations going on at the same time on these Pacific shores, commemorating our first quarter century's work. If the spirit of revivals should bless us as it has blessed Campton in the century past, bringing the intellect, the enterprise, and the wealth into the service of the Redeemer's cause here, even in a similar proportion to what it did there, it would be a great power in behalf of the salvation of the world.

Grand old Campton church! With such a history behind her for a hundred years, may her usefulness be proportionally greater in all the hundred years to come.

With sentiments of filial love, I am,

S. H. WILLEY.

CHRONOLOGICAL LIST OF MEMBERS,

BEGINNING WITH THE MEMBERS IN 1800.

In the following Table, husbands' names are in parentheses (). A female's maiden name in parentheses () indicates that she united with the church before marriage; in brackets [], after marriage.

No.	NAME.	DATE AND MANNER OF RECEPTION.	DATE AND MANNER OF REMOVAL.
1	Nathaniel Tupper		July 11, 1825 — Dis. to Ch. in Thornton.
2	Hannah [Fox] Tupper (Nathaniel)		1811 — By death.
3	Jonathan Burbank		1807 — Dis. to Bap. Ch., Campton Village.
4	Betsey [Thurlow] Burbank (Jonathan)		1807 — Dis. to Bap. Ch., Campton Village.
5	David Bartlett (Dea. 1801)	Profession	Aug. 31, 1844 — By death, aged 83.
6	Josiah Blaisdell	"	1807 — Dis. to Bap. Ch., Campton Village.
7	Deborah [ ] Spencer (Asa) Willey (Jesse)	"	1823 — By death.
8	William Baker (Dea.)		Nov. 28, 1814 — " aged 79.
9	Sarah [Brown] Baker (William)		Dec. 1814 — " "
10	Daniel Wyatt (Dea. 1815)		1821 — " "
11	Joshua Rogers		Nov. 8, 1818 — " aged 79.
12	Peletiah Chapin (Rev.)	May 25, 1800 — By letter	1807 — Dis. to Bap. Ch., Campton Village.
13	Sarah [ ] Chapin (Peletiah)		1807 — do. do.
14	Sally Chapin		1807 — do. do.
15	Darius Willey	Profession	Mar. 3, 1829 — By death, aged 91.
16	Ellice [Burbank] Cone (Thomas)		June 25, 1855 — " aged 78.
17	Huldah (Brown) Hart (Dan.)		May 1, 1834 — Dismissed.

8

CHRONOLOGICAL LIST OF MEMBERS.—*Continued.*

No.	Name.	Date and Manner of Reception.		Date and Manner of Removal.	
18	Sarah [Pulsifer] Fletcher (Joshua)	. . . . .	Profession	. . . . .	By death.
19	Mary [Willey] Willey (Darius)	June 27, 1800	"	Mar. 19, 1819	" aged 70.
20	Sarah [Merrill] Cook (Ephraim)	Oct. 26, 1800	"	Jan. 1815	"
21	Moses Baker	Dec. 7, 1800	"	Apr. 1802	"
22	Deborah [Davis] Baker (Moses)	"	"	Aug. 6, 1825	"
23	Joanna [Hazeltine] Bartlett David, Dea.	"	"	Oct. 1, 1825	"
24	Abigail [Burbeck] Noyes (Samuel) Hall (Jesse)	"	"	Feb. 12, 1843	" aged 70.
25	Isaac Fox	"	"	. . . . .	"
26	Sarah [Norris] Baker (Benjamin) Rogers (Joshua)	May 8, 1801	"	June, 1848	" aged 90.
27	David Wooster (Dea. 1801)	Aug. 28, 1801	"	1807	Dis. to Bap. Ch., Campton Village.
28	Ruth [Baker] Southmayd (John)	Oct. 23, 1801	"	1807	Dis. to Bap. Ch., Campton Village.
29	Olive [Taylor] Durgin (Asa)	"	"	. . . . .	By death.
30	James Burbeck · Dec. 1810	"	"	Mar. 17, 1844	" aged 81.
31	Elizabeth [Butler] Burbeck (James)	"	"	Mar. 22, 1844	" aged 78.
32	Joseph Burbeck	"	"	Oct. 23, 1836	Dismissed.
33	Isaac Fox, 2d	"	"	1807	Dis. to Bap. Ch., Campton Village.
34	Sarah [Taylor] Whitney (Otis)	Feb. 21, 1802	"	Mar. 20, 1826	Exc.
35	Tristram Bartlett	Apr. 23, 1802	"	Mar. 1840	By death, aged 72.
36	Abigail [Willey] Pulsifer (Joseph)	June 27, 1802	"	July 6, 1845	" aged 74.
37	Martha [Taylor] Palmer (Joseph)	Aug. 27, 1902	"	July 6, 1855	" aged 94.
38	Statira Spencer	Aug. 30, 1807	"	Sept. 26, 1843	Exc.

No.	Name		When Received	Mode	When Removed	Remarks
39	Elizabeth Palmer	...	"	"	Sept. 20, 1825	By death, aged 44.
40	Sarah [Poor] Butler (John)	...	"	"	Feb. 1843	"
41	Abel Willey	...	"	"	Mar. 20, 1834	" aged 85.
42	Mary [Burbeck] Baker (Wm. Jr.) Colburn (Peter)	...		From Ch. in Hebron	.	" aged 71.
43	Abigall [Annable] Wyatt (Daniel 2d)	...	July 17, 1808	Profession	Mar. 15, 1858	Dismissed.
44	Eunice [Cook] Marsh (Edmund)	...	Jan. 14, 1816	"	Nov. 16, 1833	By death, aged 55.
45	Hannah [Tupper] Woodbury (Benjamin)	...	"	"	May, 1823	"
46	Molly [Wyatt] Baker (Moses, Jr.)	...	"	"	Aug. 22, 1829	Dis. to Boscawen.
47	Mary (Willey) Taylor (James)	...	"	"	June, 1815	Dis. to Laconia.
48	Hannah (Bartlett) Coffin (Thomas)	...	"	"	Feb. 26, 1835	Dismissed.
49	Betsey (Butler) Cook (Moses)	...	Jan. 14, 1816	Profession	Nov 30, 1853	"
50	Miriam Willey	...	"	"	Mar. 1820	
51	Thomas Marsh	...	"	"	" "	
52	Eliza (Willey) Marsh (Thomas)	...	"	"	June, 1859	By death at Sanford, Me., aged 64.
53	Christopher Marsh (Rev. 1823)	...	"	"	Dec. 19, 1833	Dis. to Lowell, Mass.
54	Judith (Marsh) Woodman (Stephen)	...	"	"	Apr. 18, 1832	Dismissed.
55	William Baker, 3d	...	"	"		
56	Diadate Willey (Dea. 1826)	...	"	"		
57	Mary (Butler) Willey (Diadate Dea.)	...	Mar. 31, 1816	"	Feb. 1823	Dismissed.
58	Sophia (Marsh) Belcher ( )	...	"	"	June, 1850	By death.
59	Lydia Hale	...	"	"	Feb. 1871	"
60	Joanna (Bartlett) Noyes (Elijah)	...	"	"	1831	Dis. to Newbury, Mass.
61	Rebecca (Bartlett) Moody (Nathaniel)	...	"	"	Dec. 12, 1845	By death, aged 87.
62	Edmund Marsh	...	"	"		

CHRONOLOGICAL LIST OF MEMBERS, — *Continued.*

No.	Name.	Date and Manner of Reception.	Date and Manner of Removal.
63	Washington Marsh	Mar. 31, 1816 Profession	Feb. 1827 Dis. to Hardwick, Vt.
64	Rhoda [Willey] Marsh (Washington)	" "	" " "
65	David Bartlett, Jr.	" "	
66	Eunice (Marsh) Bartlett (David, Jr.)	" "	
67	Isaac Willey, Jr. (Rev. 1826)	" "	Mar. 7, 1869 Dis. to Pembroke.
68	Leonard Willey	" "	Sept. 5, 1824 By death, Williams C.
69	Mehitabel E. (Willey) Ford (Joseph)	" "	Nov. 30, 1859 "
70	Moses, Baker, Jr.	" "	May 31, 1829 " aged 60.
71	Sarah Noyes	" "	Aug. 1819 "
72	William Rogers	" "	Apr. 15, 1846 Exc.
73	Moses Cook	" "	Nov. 30, 1853 Dis. to Laconia.
74	John Rogers	" "	July 15, 1859 Dis. to Lowell, Mass.
75	Abigail (Burbeck) Rogers (John)	" "	" " "
76	Lydia (Burbeck) Little (William)	June 23, 1816 "	Apr. 14, 1832 Dismissed.
77	Joseph Ford	" "	July 10, 1856 By death.
78	Ebenezer Little, Jr.	" "	Sept. 1, 1837 Dismissed.
79	Jacob Giddings	" "	Oct. 1834 "
80	Leonard Rogers (Rev.)	" "	
81	John Wooster (Rev. 1834)	" "	Dec. 4, 1873 By death.
82	Esther (Church) Colby (William)	" "	May 6, 1858 "
83	Lydia S. Willey	" "	Jan. 18, 1817 "

No.	Name	Admitted		Removed	Dis. to Ch. in Dover.
84	Mary (Pulsifer) Cook (William)	"	"	Feb. 19, 1840	Dis. to Ch. in Dover.
85	Nehemiah Brown	Aug. 18, 1816	"	Feb. 1818	Dismissed.
86	Lydia [Worcester] Brown (Nehemiah)	"	"	" "	"
87	Hannah [Palmer] Blair (Peter)	"	"	Mar. 23, 1817	By death.
88	Edmund Cook	"	"	Apr. 25, 1862	"
89	Clarissa [Mitchell] Cook (Edmund)	"	"	Aug. 9, 1856	"
90	Jerusha (Little) Cummings (Charles)	"	"	Feb. 5, 1827	Dismissed.
91	Samuel Elliott	"	"	July 11, 1825	"
92	William Johnson	"	"	Apr. 10, 1828	By death.
93	George W. Elliott (Rev. 1825)	"	"	June, 1825	By death.
94	Susanna (Foss) Durgin (Francis)	Oct. 6, 1816	"	Dec. 29, 1833	Dismissed.
95	Sarah (Burbeck) Orr (William)	"	"	July 6, 1819	By death.
96	Robert Morrison	Dec. 22, 1816	"	June 30, 1853	"
97	Otis Whitney	"	"	Feb. 1825	Dismissed.
98	Abigail (Willey) Brown (Samuel)	"	By letter	Feb. 1822	"
99	Amos P. Brown (Rev. Jan. 1817)	Jan. 1, 1817	Profession	Jan. 7, 1849	By death.
100	Darius Willey, Jr.	Feb. 9, 1817	"	Sept. 12, 1859	Dismissed.
101	Mary [Pulsifer] Willey (Darius, Jr.)	"	"	May, 1845	"
102	Charity (Willey) Ladd (James)	"	"	Oct. 23, 1836	By death.
103	Anna [Ford] Morrison (Robert)	"	"	June, 1860	"
104	Esther [Willey] Houston (David)	"	"	1854	"
105	Sarah Ferrin	"	"		
106	Mary (Burbeck) Ladd (Arnold)	"	"		
107	Moses Clark	"	"	Nov. 22, 1818	Exc.

CHRONOLOGICAL LIST OF MEMBERS.—*Continued.*

NO.	NAME.	DATE AND MANNER OF RECEPTION.		DATE AND MANNER OF REMOVAL.	
108	Israel Spencer	Feb. 9, 1817	Profession	Sept. 26, 1813	Exc.
109	Molly [Tupper] Spencer (Israel)	"	"	Aug. 4, 1850	Dis. to Bap. Ch., Campton Village.
110	Margaret [Bump] Woodbury (Joseph)	Mar. 16, 1817	"	Feb. 6, 1861	By death, aged 84.
111	Rebecca (Baker) Cook (Coffin)	"	"	Mar. 25, 1838	"
112	Daniel Pulsifer (Rev. 1834)	July 13, 1817	"	May 6, 1844	Dis. to Ch. in Danbury.
113	John Pulsifer	Nov. 24, 1817	"	Aug. 19, 1874	By death, aged 93.
114	Ruth (Butler) Durgin (Francis)	Jan. 11, 1818	"	May, 1834	Dis. to Bap. Ch., Campton Village.
115	Lucy [Ford] Burbank (Ebenezer)	Sept. 13, 1818	By letter	Oct. 1834	Dismissed.
116	Jane [Little] Brown (Amos P. Rev.)	Aug. 1820	"	......	By death.
117	James Ladd	Aug. 1820	Profession	May, 1845	Dismissed.
118	John W. Kimball	Jan. 1821	By letter	May, 1846	Dis. to Beaver Dam, Wis.
119	Ebenezer B. rlett.	June 13, 1824	From ch. in Plymouth	Mar. 1, 1840	By death.
120	Mary [Hobart] Lovejoy ( ) Bartlett (Ebenezer),	"	"	......	"
121	John Clark, Jr.	"	"	July 13, 1836	Exc.
122	Sarah [Cook] Clark (John, Jr.)	"	"	Dec. 20, 1837	"
123	Moody Cook	"	"	Dec. 31, 1834	By death, aged 84.
124	Edmund Cook, 2d	"	"	May, 1819	Dis. to Lowell, Mass.
125	Electa [Bartlett] Cook (Edmund, 2d)	"	"	" "	"
126	Lydia Cook	"	"	......	By death.
127	Lucy [Eaton] Cook (Moody, Jr.)	"	"	Mar. 1, 1809	" aged 78.
128	Eliza [Bartlett] Morrison (Ebenezer B.)	"	"	June 9, 1861	"

No.	Name	Admitted	Mode	Removed	Remarks
129	Sarah [Bartlett] Cook (Ephraim, Jr.)	"	"	Mar. 9, 1862	"
130	Eleanor [Marsh] Palmer (Dudley, Jr.)	"	"	. . . .	"
131	Sarah [Lambkin] Mills (Stone)	"	"	1837	Dismissed.
132	Jonathan L. Hale (Rev. 1824)	June 27, 1824	By letter	April, 1832	"
133	Phebe [Palmer] Little (Ebenezer)	Sept. 5, 1824	Profession	May, 1837	"
134	Hannah [Cook] Clark (Joseph)	"	"	1832	By death.
135	Fanny [Harvey] Hale (Jonathan L., Rev.)	Jan. 9, 1825	By letter	Jan. 3, 1832	"
136	Herrey Johnson	Mar. 1825	"	Sept. 24, 1835	Dismissed.
137	Sarah [De Forest] Johnson (Hervey)	"	"	Nov. 22, 1831	By death.
138	Susan [Ryan] Willey (Isaac)	July 17, 1825	Profession	1863	"
139	Mary [Blaisdell] Baker (Wm. 3d)	"	"	April, 1832	Dismissed.
140	Rachel Chase	"	"	Mar. 1, 1844	By death.
141	Rhoda Chase	"	"	June 30, 1867	"
142	Moody Cook, Jr.	"	"	May 29, 1855	"
143	James Merrill	"	"	Jan. 13, 1840	"
144	Sarah [Foss] Merrill (James)	"	"	May, 1872	"
145	Rebecca [Pingree] Palmer (Dudley)	"	"	Dec. 24, 1834	"
146	Appha [Palmer] Clark (Joseph)	"	"	Mar. 16, 1843	Exc.
147	Joseph Clark	Oct. 2, 1825	"	"	"
148	John Clark, 4th (Rev. 1834)	"	"	1830	Dismissed.
149	William Cook	"	"	Feb. 19, 1840	Dis. to Ch. in Dover.
150	James Little	"	"	Apr. 22, 1838	Dismissed.
151	Polly [Cook] Little (James)	"	"	"	"
152	Davis Baker	"	"	June, 1842	By death.

CHRONOLOGICAL LIST OF MEMBERS,—*Continued.*

No.	Name.	Date and Manner of Reception.		Date and Manner of Removal.	
153	Hannah [Church] Baker (Davis)	Oct. 2, 1825	Profession	Oct. 1843	By death.
154	Martha [Bartlett] Cook (Thomas)	"	"	Aug. 30, 1859	"
155	Arvilla (Cook) Spencer (Henry)	"	"	Feb. 9, 1853	Dismissed.
156	Alvira (Lovejoy) Foss (Leonard)	"	"	July 17, 1845	Dis. to Ch. in Thornton.
157	Sally [Cook] Taylor (Enoch)	"	From F. W.B.Ellsworth		
158	Mary Giddings	"	Profession	Mar. 2, 1869	By death, aged 97.
159	Ebenezer B. Morrison	Nov. 20, 1825	"	Mar. 12, 1876	"
160	Coffin Cook	"	"	May, 1865	"
161	John Chandler (Dea. 1844)	"	"	Mar. 11, 1856	"
162	Clarissa Chandler	"	"	1834	"
163	Hepsibah (Palmer) Clark (Amos)	"	"		
164	Mary L. (Blair) Johnson (Nathan M.)	"	"	Oct. 8, 1867	By death.
165	Ephraim Cook, Jr.	Jan. 15, 1826	"	1861	Dis. to Wentworth.
166	Hannah [Dearborn] Cook (Ephraim, Jr.)	"	"	Oct. 4, 1827	By death.
167	Harriet Percival	"	"	Aug. 16, 1830	"
168	Caroline (Cook) Holmes (John)	Mar. 19, 1826	"	Nov. 24, 1847	Exc.
169	Isaac Farnham	May 21, 1826	"	Feb. 3, 1853	Dis. to Lowell, Mass.
170	Fanny [ ] Graham ( ) Farnham (Isaac)	"	"	" "	"
171	Jonathan Glines	"	"		
172	Eliza [Noyes] Glines (Jonathan)	"	"	Dec. 1, 1856	By death.
173	Austin Willey (Rev.1859)	"	"	Aug. 19, 1840	Dis. to Hallowell, Me.

174	Lois (Baker) Blair (William H.)	July 23, 1826	"	July 10, 1846	By death.
175	Mary [Baker] Keniston (John)	Sept. 17, 1826	"	1849	Dis. to Plymouth.
176	Anna [Burbeck] Blaisdell (Nathaniel)	Nov. 19, 1826	"	1870	Dis. to F. W. B., Barnstead.
177	Lucy (Coleman) Page (Calvin)	" "	"	Nov. 1830	Dismissed.
178	Abigail (Coleman) Page (Calvin)	" "	"	May, 1834	"
179	Polly [Palmer] Pulsifer (John)	July 29, 1827	"	Apr. 30, 1832	By death.
180	Eliza Bartlett	" "	"	......	"
181	William Henry Blair	Oct. 28, 1827	Profession	Dec. 8, 1856	By death.
182	Worcester Willey (Rev. 1844)	"	"	May, 1834	Dismissed.
183	John P. Hayes	"	"	......	Unknown.
184	Caroline Pulsifer	"	"	May 10, 1840	Dis. to Lowell, Mass.
185	Adaline (Willey) Aiken (Charles)	"	"	1840	Dismissed.
186	Eleanor [ ] Towle ( ) Bartlett (David, Dea.)	Mar. 2, 1828	From Haverhill	......	By death.
187	Alice [Merrill] Baker (Daniel) Johnson (Hervey)	July 20, 1828	Profession	Sept. 28, 1835	Dismissed.
188	Polly (Baker) Taylor (Gilman R.)	Sept. 28, 1828	"	June 29, 1864	By death.
189	Judith R. (Bartlett) Willey (Austin, Rev.)	July 19, 1829	"	Aug. 19, 1840	Dis. to Hallowell, Me.
190	Emeline Sanborn	" "	"	......	Unknown.
191	Sally (Colby) Jackson (Henry)	Sept. 22, 1829	"	Sept. 25, 1873	Dis. to Bowdoin St. Ch., Boston.
192	Hall Robertson	Jan. 10, 1830	"	1936	Dismissed.
193	Eliza K. [ ] Robertson (Hall)	" "	"	"	"
194	Sarah [Gilbert] Moody (Joseph)	May, 1831	"	May 3, 1873	"
195	Susanna K. (Coleman) Holmes (James)	July 31, 1831	Profession	Sept. 1834	"
196	Joseph Coleman Blair	July 31, 1831	"	Oct. 29, 1864	By death.
197	Anna [Ryan] Burbeck (Joseph)	Oct. 2, 1831	"	Oct. 23, 1836	Dismissed.

9

CHRONOLOGICAL LIST OF MEMBERS. — *Continued.*

No.	Name.	Date and Manner of Reception.		Date and Manner of Removal.	
198	Elizabeth [Pulsifer] Giddings (Jacob)	Oct. 2. 1831	Profession	Oct. 1834	Dismissed.
199	Abigail (Colburn) Sawyer ( ) George (Thomas)	" "	"	1834	"
200	Ezra W. Avery	Dec. 4, 1831	"	Jan. 22, 1845	Exc.
201	Ruth [Bucknam] Avery (Ezra W.)	" "	"	May 6, 1844	Dis. to Ch. in Danbury.
202	Betsey (Stevens) Pulsifer (Daniel, Rev.)	" "	"	May 6, 1844	Dis. to Ch. in Danbury.
203	Martha (Pulsifer) Wyatt (George W.)	" "	"	Jan. 1840	Dis. to Ch. in Charlestown, Mass.
204	Dolly (Noyes) Blair (Joseph C.)	" "	"		
205	Martha (Marsh) Thurston (Josiah)	" "	"	April, 1834	Dis. to Bap. Ch., Campton Village.
206	Lydia Houston	" "	"		By death.
207	Hannah (Higgins) George (Moses)	" "	"		"
208	Harriet (Wyatt) Homan (E. Rockwood)	" "	"		
209	Sarah (Merrill) Holmes (Wm. B.) Burbeck (Sam'l N.)	" "	"	1874	Dis. to Ch., Westford, Mass.
210	Caroline (Merrill) Pray ( )	" "	"		Dismissed to Lowell.
211	Abigail P. Butler	" "	"	April, 1834	Dis. to Bap. Ch., Campton Village.
212	Harriet (Cook) Dole (John)	" "	"	May 4, 1856	Dis. to Ch. in Bangor, Me.
213	Selden C. Willey	" "	"		
214	Emeline Willey	" "	"	Dec. 5, 1833	By death.
215	Almira (Farnham) Adams (Joseph)	" "	"	Nov. 1833	Dismissed.
216	Jane Graham	" "	"	" "	"
217	Adeline (Morrison) Merrill (Gardner)	" "	"	July 10, 1843	Exc.
218	Sally P. (Coleman) Sanborn ( )	" "	"	Sept. 1834	Dismissed.

No.	Name					Remarks
210	Harriet P. De Forest	"	"		1833	"
220	Lucy Woodbury	July 15, 1834	"		May 28, 1816	By death.
221	Abigail Pulsifer	"	"		July 5, 1862	"
222	Applia [Fessenden] Stone (Benj. P., Rev., D.D.)	"	By letter		Nov. 21, 1839	Dis. to Ch. in Concord.
223	Thankful [Olmsted] Ladd (Jesse)	"	"		June 10, 1845	By death.
224	Mary Ann (Cook) Dole (Henry)	Jan. 4, 1835	Profession		Feb. 15, 1842	Dis. to Limerick, Me.
225	Sally P. (Cook) Cook (Joseph)	"	"		Feb. 13, 1847	By death.
226	George W. Wyatt	Mar. 1, 1835	"		Jan. 1840	Dis. to Ch. in Charlestown, Mass.
227	Carr Chase	"	"		Nov. 23, 1836	Dismissed.
228	Joanna [Huse] Chase (Carr)	"	"		" "	"
229	Daniel M. Huse	"	"			"
230	Eliza [Dudley] Huse (Daniel M.)	"	"			"
231	Sally (McAllister) Leuce (Calvin)	"	"			
232	Newton Marsh	"	"		Apr. 13, 1875	By death, aged 73.
233	Lydia H. [Butler] Marsh (Newton)	"	"		Aug. 4, 1850	Dis. to Bap. Ch., Campton Village.
234	Mary (Spencer) Blaisdell (Charles)	"	"		May, 1837	Dismissed.
235	Mary Little	"	"			
236	Sarah (Cook) Burbank (William)	"	"		May, 1846	Dismissed.
237	Samuel H. Willey (Rev. 1848, D.D.)	"	"		May, 1846	Dismissed.
238	Elizabeth L. (Noyes) Baker (Walter W.)	May 3, 1835	"		Nov. 10, 1847	"
239	Martha Ann (Noyes) Blair (Nathan H.)	"	"		Dec. 9, 1867	By death.
240	Annette (Willey) Cook (Jason Dea.)	"	"			
241	Louise (Cook) Harwood (Ephraim)	May 3, 1835	Profession		July 5, 1840	Dis. to 3d Cong. Ch., Lowell, Mass.
242	Charles Little	"	"		May, 1837	Dismissed.

CHRONOLOGICAL LIST OF MEMBERS,—*Continued.*

No.	Name.	Date and Manner of Reception.		Date and Manner of Removal.
243	Caroline (Merrill) Page (Edwin)	May 3, 1835	Profession	Nov. 14, 1842	Dis. to Ch. in Lowell, Mass.
244	Mary Bartlett	Sept. 4, 1836	"	Sept. 12, 1851	By death.
245	Statira (Spencer) Baker (Davis, Jr.)	"	"	July 3, 1843	Exc.
246	Hannah [French] Cook (Alvin)	"	"	Nov. 1842	By death.
247	Mark Marden	Jan. 1, 1837	"	1888	Dis. F. W. B., Epsom.
248	Walter W. Baker	May 6, 1838	"	Nov. 10, 1847	Dismissed.
249	Davis Baker, Jr.	" "	"	July 3, 1843	Exc.
250	Thomas P. Beach (Rev.)	" "	By letter	Sept. 6, 1841	"
251	Daniel Pillsbury	" "	From Plymouth	Jan. 5, 1840	Dis. to Newbury, Mass.
252	Sarah (Cook) Little (Moses)	July 1, 1838	Profession	Oct. 14, 1838	Dismissed.
253	Catherine (Cook) Cook (Alvin) Hatch (Albert)	" "	"	May, 1849	Dis. to 1st Cong. Ch., Lowell, Mass.
254	Elihu C. Baker	Sept. 2, 1838	"	May 22, 1844	Exc.
255	Sarah [Baker] Beach (Thomas P., Rev.)	Nov. 4, 1838		Dec. 19, 1855	Dismissed.
256	Harriet [Little] Noyes (Benjamin)	Dec. 19, 1838	From Plymouth	Mar. 16, 1857	By death.
257	Zebedee Cook	Jan. 6, 1839	Profession	Feb. 13, 1868	Dis. Mantorville, Minn.
258	Joseph Pulsifer, Jr.	" "	"	Mar. 27, 1861	By death, aged 46.
259	Betsey [Burleigh] Pillsbury (Daniel)	" "	"	Jan. 5, 1840	Dis. to ch. in Newbury.
260	Gardner Merrill	" "	"	July 10, 1843	Exc.
261	Elizabeth Pulsifer	" "	"	May 11, 1850	By death.
262	Hannah (Baker) Spencer (Gardiner)	" "	"	Dec. 18, 1844	Exc.
263	Joseph Pulsifer	Mar. 3, 1839	"	Aug. 11, 1851	By death, aged 81.

No.	Name	Date	From / Profession	Date	Remarks
264	Phebe [Pulsifer] Stickney (Benjamin)	"	From Ch., Newb'ry, Ms.	Nov. 19, 1861	By death.
265	George Spencer	May 5, 1839	Profession		
266	Sarah [Bartlett] Johnson (William) Spencer (Geo.)	"	"	Dec. 7, 1859	Dis. to Ch. in Manchester.
267	Hazen Sanborn	"	"	1870	Dis. to F. W. B.
268	Ann [Marel] Sanborn (Hazen)	"	"	1870	" "
269	Elvira (Holmes) Howell ( )	"	"	Sept. 2), 1843	Dis. to Ch. in Hadlyme, Conn.
270	Jane [Burbeck] Chandler (John, Dea.)	"	"	June 20, 1865	By death.
271	Elizabeth G. [Burbeck] Rogers (William)	"	"	Apr. 15, 1846	Exc.
272	Moses George	July 5, 1840	From Newbury, Mass.		By death.
273	Sarah [Danforth] George (Moses)	"	"		
274	Jane [Clough] Spencer (Nathaniel)	Jan. 21, 1841	From Old South, Boston	Aug. 4, 1850	Dis. to Bap. Ch., Campton Village.
275	Elizabeth [Denison] Willey (Selden, C.)	Feb. 24, 1841	Frm Tab. Ch. Salem, Ms.	Mar. 26, 1846	By death.
276	Eliza [Rowel] Shedd (Charles, Rev.)	Feb. 1842	By letter	Mar. 29, 1857	Dis. to Zumbrota, Minn.
277	Martha L. [Foss] Pulsifer (John)	Mar. 25, 1842	From Hopkinton		
278	Caroline E. (Rowel) Skinner (A. G.)	Aug. 17, 1842	By letter		Dismissed.
279	Elizabeth (Cutter) Howe (Lucius M.)	July 7, 1844	"	Sept. 25, 1860	By death.
280	John M. Hodge	"	Profession	May 31, 1848	Exc.
281	Abigail [Dole] Kimball (John W.)	Aug. 21, 1844	By letter		Dis. to Beaver Dam, Wis.
282	Mehitabel [Hutchins] Tucker (Luther) Clark (John) Morse (Stephen)	Apr. 14, 1845	From Plymouth		By death.
283	Susan [Hobart] Johnson (David)	"	"	Dec. 1843	"
284	Sally [Johnson] Draper (Reuben)	"	"	July, 1867	"
285	Jesse A. Sanborn	Dec. 1, 1846	By letter	Mar. 29, 1871	Dis. to Presb. Ch., Mankato Minn.
286	Sarah [Sanborn] Sanborn (Jesse A.)	"	"	Dec. 1870	"
287	Mary [Hosley] Cutter (John T.)	"	"	July 12, 1854	Dis. to ch. in Plymouth.

CHRONOLOGICAL LIST OF MEMBERS, — *Continued.*

No.	NAME.	DATE AND MANNER OF RECEPTION.	DATE AND MANNER OF REMOVAL.	
288	Henry E. Shedd	Nov. 7, 1847 Profession	Oct. 29, 1849	Dismissed.
289	Caroline L. (Butler) Shedd (Henry E.)	" "	Apr. 13, 1854	Dis. to Payson Ch., Boston.
290	Alpheus Chandler	" "	June 3, 1849	Dismissed.
291	William A. Hodge	" "	" "	Dis. to Bap. Ch., Campton Village.
292	Eliza A. C. (Rogers) Chase (Walter, Rev.)	" "	Nov. 20, 1850	Dis. to Bap. Ch., Campton Village.
293	Joseph Chandler	Jan. 9, 1848	Apr. 21, 1850	Dismissed.
294	Elizabeth (Cook) Sargent ( ) Auson (George)	July 2, 1848	Nov. 30, 1853	Dis. to Ch. in Laconia.
295	Moses Pulsifer	Jan. 7, 1849	May 31, 1855	By death.
296	David B. Pulsifer	" "		
297	M. Melvina [Harvey] Willey (S. C.)	" "		
298	Mary W. Taylor	Nov. 3, 1850	Sept. 14, 1852	By death.
299	Mary E. (Moses) Reed (Wm. H.)	Nov. 7, 1852	Nov. 18, 1861	Dis. to Ch. in Plymouth.
300	William Colby (Dea. 1856)	Dec. 22, 1852 From Ch. in Morgan, Vt.		By death.
301	Henry D. Wyatt	Jan. 2, 1853 Profession		
302	Amanda H. (Blaisdell) Coburn (William)	Jan. 2, 1853 "	Aug. 5, 1860	Dis. to Park Street Ch., Boston.
303	Hannah B. (Burbeck) Wallace (William)	" "		
304	M. Elizabeth Shedd	" "	Mar. 29, 1857	Dis. to Zumbrota, Min.
305	Hannah B. (Pulsifer) Brown (Wm. G., Dea.)	Mar. 4, 1853 By letter.		
306	Annette [Blaisdell] Goss (Daniel F. A.)	Mar. 6, 1853 Profession	Nov. 2, 1866	Dis. to Tab. Ch., Salem, Mass.
307	Gilman R. Smith	" "		
308	Adaline H. (Burbeck) Smith (Gilman, R.)	May 1, 1853 "		

No.	Name	Received		Date	Disposition
309	Calvin Louee		"	Dec. 10, 1872	By death, aged 63
310	William G. Cook		"	Feb. 1854	Dis. to Ch. in Plym'uth.
311	Jason Cook (Dea. 1861)		"	Mar. 3, 1871	By death.
312	Cyrus Burbeck		"	Aug. 7, 1863	" at Chicago, on his ret. from war.
313	John Chandler, Jr.		"	Aug. 18, 1858	Exc.
314	Daniel Wyatt		"		
315	Sarah Ann Durgin		"		
316	Jane B. (Little) Palmer (Samuel H.)		"		
317	Hannah P. (Johnson) Gale (John)		"		
318	Malvina (Cook) Pulsifer (Charles W.)		"		
319	Martha B. (Moses) Stanton (Chas. P.)		"		
320	Nancy A. (Moses) Cox (William W., Jr.)		"		
321	Samuel Chandler	July 3, 1853	"	July 5, 1856	Dis. to Presb. Ch., Milford, N. Y.
322	Moses C. Dole	Sept. 3, 1853	"		
323	Lucy (Cook) Dole (Moses C).	"	"		
324	Clarissa [Baker] Cook (Zebedee)	"	"		
325	William Judson Greenough	"	"		
326	Mary F. Whitney	Jan. 1, 1854	"	Jan. 11, 1860	By death.
327	Hannah Cook	"	"	Aug. 1868	By death.
328	Samantha [Cook] Dole (Erastus)	Jan. 7, 1855	'		
329	Clarissa S. (Flint) Cook (Henry)	July 6, 1856	"	July 17, 1858	By death.
330	Isabella W. [Draper] Pulsifer (David B.)	Oct. 30, 1856	By letter		
331	William G. Brown (Dea. 1861)	Dec. 17, 1856	"		
332	Louise [Cowles] Hadley (James B., Rev.)	July 18, 1858	"	June 20, 1868	By death, aged 55.

CHRONOLOGICAL LIST OF MEMBERS.—*Continued.*

No.	Name.	Date and Manner of Reception.		Date and Manner of Removal.	
333	Louise J. Hadley	By letter	July 16, 1858	Apr. 20, 1862	By death, aged 25.
334	Persis [Ruggles] Church (Ira)	"	"		
335	Sarah P. [Church] Frouk (Edwin)	"	"		
336	Martha (Bartlett) Huntress (Andrew J.)	Profession	"	Mar. 1866	Dis. to Ch., Groveland, Mass.
337	Sarah Ellen Sanborn	"	"	Dec. 1870	Dis. Pres. Ch., Mankato, Min.
338	Charles H. Willey	"	"	July, 1863	By death in the army.
339	Joseph Cook	"	Nov. 7, 1858		
340	Eliza A. [Kendrick] Cook (Joseph)	"	"		
341	Nancy L. [Howard] Flint (Amos)	From Hillsboro' Bridge.	Jan. 2, 1859		
342	Hannah P. [Cook] Pulsifer (Thos. S.)	Profession	"		
343	Thomas S. Pulsifer	"	May 1, 1859		
344	Erastus Dole	"	"		
345	Phebe Dole	"	"		
346	Ezekiel H. Hodgdon (Dea. 1873)	"	"		
347	Almira [Dole] Hodgdon (Ezekiel H., Dea.)	By letter	"		
348	Peletiah C. Blaisdell	Profession	July 3, 1859	Aug. 24, 1873	By death, age 72.
349	Benjamin Stickney	"	"		
350	Hermon C. Stickney	"	"	June 24, 1865	By death.
351	Mary E. Stickney	"	"	Apr. 3, 1870	Dis. to 2d Ch., Cambridge, Mass.
352	Armeda E. (Merrill) Bartlett (Andrew J.)	"	"		
353	Rulamah A. (Mosee) Kennedy (John H.)	"	"	Sept. 26, 1875	Dis. to Ch., Lowell, Mass.

No.	Name		Date	Source	Date	Note
354	Sarah [Merrill] Cook (Almon H.)	. . . . .	"	From Plymouth		
355	Eunice Bartlett	. . . . .	"	From Lowell		
356	Julia Ann Marsh	. . . . .	Nov. 6, 1859	Profession		
357	Christopher M. Bartlett	. . . . .	Jan. 1, 1860	"		
358	Lois [Cook] Blaisdell (Peletiah C.)	. . . . .	"	"		
359	Jane [Bryant] Homan (Gilbert W.)	. . . . .	"	By letter		
360	George Foss	. . . . .	1860	From Fisherville		
361	Deborah G. [Bryant] Foss (Geo.)	. . . . .	"	" "		
362	Lizzie H. [Elliott] Foss (Martin H.)	. . . . .	Nov. 14, 1860	By letter	Nov. 25, 1860	By death.
363	Martin H. Foss	. . . . .	Jan. 6, 1861	Profession	Apr. 7, 1872	Dis. to Tab. Ch., Chicago, Ill.
364	Emily B. (Abbot) Webber (David A.)	. . . . .	Dec. 6, 1861	By letter	Mar. 12, 1874	By death, aged 52.
365	Charles W. Pulsifer	. . . . .	Mar. 2, 1862	Profession		
366	Samuel C. Hill	. . . . .	Mar. 3, 1864	From Jamaica Plain		
367	Eliza L. [French] Hill (Sam'l C.)	. . . . .	"	" "		
368	Eldora B. (Foss) Cook (Arthur B.)	. . . . .	May 1, 1864	Profession		
369	Frances J. [Blair] Littlefield (Jas.)	. . . . .	July 3, 1864	From Kennebunk, Me.	Aug. 29, 1875	Dis. to Ch., Plymouth.
370	Gertrude [Sykes] Blakely (Quincy, Rev.)	. . . . .	"	From Rodman, N. Y.		
371	Sarah L. Pulsifer	. . . . .	"	From Lowell, Mass.		
372	Jennie [McNiece] Cone (M. Bartlett)	. . . . .	Mar. 5, 1865	From Bath		
373	Clarissa [Bartlett] Little (Henry)	. . . . .	May 7, 1865	Profession	Dec. 15, 1870	By death.
374	S. Frances (Littlefield) Thornton (William)	. . . . .	"	"		
375	Amanda S. (Webber) Kennedy (John H.)	. . . . .	"	"	Aug. 13, 1883	By death.
376	Lydia [Keniston] Baron (Oliver, Rev.)	. . . . .	Sept. 2, 1866	From Appleton Street, Lowell		
377	Charles C. Joslyn	. . . . .	Nov. 4, 1866	From Deering		

10

CHRONOLOGICAL LIST OF MEMBERS,—*Continued.*

NO.	NAME.	DATE AND MANNER OF RECEPTION.		DATE AND MANNER OF REMOVAL.	
378	Ellen A. Cole	Jan. 6, 1867	From So. Ch., Concord.		
379	Joseph Henry Brown	May 5, 1867	Profession	June 11, 1871	Dis. to Ch. in Hyde Park, Mass.
380	M. Carrie (Blair) Tirrell (Fred N.)	" "	"		
381	Laura A. Blair	" "	"		
382	Frances L. (Chase) Little (George H.)	" "	"		
383	Clara Osgood	" "	"		
384	Emily E. Webber	" "	From F. W. B., W. Campton	Sept. 8, 1870	By death.
385	Isaac S. Moses	" "	"		
386	Margaret [Morrison] Moses (Isaac S.)	" "	"		
387	Jennie B. [Burleigh] Blair (Joseph C.)	" "	From F. W. B., Haverhill, Mass.		
388	Pamelia H. (Homan) Mitchell (Samuel S.)	" "	From Roxbury, Mass.		
389	Emma F. (Evans) Evans (Darius)	July 7, 1867	Profession		
390	Elizabeth P. (Hodgdon) Elliott (Lester H., Rev.)	Sept. 1, 1867	"		
391	William Wallace	Jan. 5, 1868	From Wentworth		
392	William H. Stickney	Nov. 1, 1868	Profession		
393	Edwin H. Stickney	" "	"		
394	Moody C. Dole	" "	"		
395	Horatio H. Thornton	Jan. 3, 1869	"		
396	John Mason Blaisdell	July 3, 1870	"		
397	Julia A. (Hall) Blaisdell (John M.)	" "	"		

398	Charles O. Stickney	"	"	Dec. 24, 1873	Dis. to Ch., E st., Boston, Mass.
399	Esther E. Willey	"	"	June 14, 1873	By death.
400	Bessie E. [George] Moulton (Gideon H.)	"	From M.E.Ch., Plym'th,		
401	Hester [Elliott] Johnson (Melvin H.)	Nov. 3, 1872	From Bap. Ch., Lowell.		
402	Laura A. [Eaton] Stickney (Benj. F.)	Mar. 1, 1874	From M. E. Ch., Lowell.		
403	Sarah F. Cook	Sept. 6, 1874	Profession		
404	Harriet A. Hodgdon	Jan. 3, 1875	"		
405	H. Louise [Stevens] Clark (Theodore P.)	"	"		
406	George W. Wallace	"	From Bath		
407	Gilman R. Taylor	Jan. 3, 1875	From M.E.Ch., Plym'th.		
408	Sarah E. [Blair] Dole (Moses C.)	May 2, 1875	Profession		
409	Norris Holmes	July 4, 1875	"		
410	George B. Foss	"	"		

ALPHABETICAL LIST.

THE NUMBERS REFER TO THE CHRONOLOGICAL LIST.

215 Adams, Almira F.
185 Aiken, Adaline W.
200 Avery, Ezra W.
201 Avery, Ruth B.

8 Baker, William.
9 Baker, Sarah B.
21 Baker, Moses.
22 Baker, Deborah D.
70 Baker, Moses, Jr.
46 Baker, Molly W.
55 Baker, William, 3d.
139 Baker, Mary B.
152 Baker, Davis.
153 Baker, Hannah C.
248 Baker, Walter W.
238 Baker, Elizabeth L.
249 Baker, Davis, Jr.
245 Baker, Satira S.
254 Baker, Elihu C.
376 Baron, Lydia K.
5 Bartlett, David.
23 Bartlett, Joanna H.
186 Bartlett, Eleanor.
35 Bartlett, Tristram.
65 Bartlett, David, Jr.
66 Bartlett, Eunice M.
119 Bartlett, Ebenezer.
120 Bartlett, Mary H.
180 Bartlett, Eliza.
244 Bartlett, Mary.
352 Bartlett, Armeda E.
355 Bartlett, Eunice.
357 Bartlett, Christopher M.
250 Beach, Thomas P.
255 Beach, Sarah B.
58 Belcher, Sophia M.
87 Blair, Hannah P.
181 Blair, William H.
174 Blair, Lois B.
196 Blair, Joseph C.
204 Blair, Dolly N.
239 Blair, Martha Ann N.
381 Blair, Laura A.
387 Blair, Jennie S.
6 Blaisdell, Josiah.
176 Blaisdell, Anna B.
234 Blaisdell, Mary S.
348 Blaisdell Pelotiah C.
358 Blaisdell, Lois C.
396 Blaisdell. John M.
397 Blaisdell, Julia A.
370 Blakely, Gertrude S.
85 Brown, Nehemiah.
86 Brown, Lydia W.
98 Brown, Abigail W.
99 Brown, Amos P.
116 Brown, Jane L.
331 Brown, William G.
305 Brown, Hannah B.
379 Brown, Joseph Henry.
3 Burbank, Jonathan.
4 Burbank, Betsey T.
115 Burbank, Lucy F.
236 Burbank, Sarah C.

30 Burbeck, James.
31 Burbeck, Elizabeth R.
32 Burbeck, Joseph.
197 Burbeck, Anna R.
209 Burbeck, Sarah M.
312 Burbeck, Cyrus.
40 Butler, Sarah P.
211 Butler, Abigail P.

161 Chandler, John.
162 Chandler, Clarissa.
270 Chandler, Jane B.
290 Chandler, Alpheus.
293 Chandler, Joseph.
313 Chandler, John, Jr.
321 Chandler, Samuel.
12 Chapin, Peletiah.
13 Chapin, Sarah.
14 Chapin, Sally.
140 Chase, Rachel.
141 Chase, Rhoda.
227 Chase, Carr.
228 Chase, Joanna H.
292 Chase, Eliza A. C.
334 Church, Persis R.
107 Clark, Moses.
121 Clark, John, Jr.
122 Clark, Sarah C.
147 Clark, Joseph.
134 Clark, Hannah C.
146 Clark, Aphia P.
148 Clark, John, 4th.
163 Clark, Hepsibah P.
405 Clark, H. Louise.
302 Coburn. Amanda H.
48 Coffin. Hannah B.
42 Colburn, Mary B.
300 Colby, William.
82 Colby, Esther C.
378 Cole, Ellen A.
16 Cone, Ellice B.
372 Cone, Jennie M.
20 Cook, Sarah M.
73 Cook, Moses.
49 Cook, Betsey B.
149 Cook, William.
84 Cook, Mary P.
88 Cook, Edmund.
89 Cook, Clarissa M.
160 Cook, Coffin.
111 Cook, Rebecca B.
123 Cook, Moody.
124 Cook, Edmund, 2d.
125 Cook, Electa B.
126 Cook, Lydia.
142 Cook, Moody, Jr.
127 Cook, Lucy E.
154 Cook, Martha B.
165 Cook, Ephraim, Jr.
166 Cook, Hannah B.
129 Cook, Sarah B.
310 Cook, William G.
311 Cook, Jason.
240 Cook, Annette W.
246 Cook, Hannah F.

257 Cook, Zebedee.
324 Cook, Clarissa B.
327 Cook, Hannah.
329 Cook, Clarissa S.
339 Cook, Joseph.
225 Cook. Sally P.
340 Cook, Eliza A.
354 Cook, Sarah M.
368 Cook, Eldora B.
403 Cook, Sarah F.
320 Cox, Nancy A.
90 Cummings, Jerusha L.
287 Cutter, Mary H.

219 De Forest, Harriet P.
212 Dole, Harriet C.
224 Dole, Mary Ann C.
322 Dole, Moses C.
323 Dole, Lucy C.
408 Dole, Sarah E.
344 Dole, Erastus.
328 Dole, Samantha C.
345 Dole, Phebe.
394 Dole, Moody C.
284 Draper, Sally J.
29 Durgin, Olive T.
94 Durgin, Susanna F.
114 Durgin, Ruth B.
315 Durgin, Sarah Ann.

91 Elliott, Samuel.
93 Elliott, George W.
390 Elliott, Elizabeth P.
389 Evans, Emma F.

169 Farnham, Isaac.
170 Farnham, Fanny.
105 Ferrin, Sarah.
18 Fletcher, Sarah P.
341 Flint, Nancy L.
77 Ford, Joseph.
69 Ford, Mehitabel E.
156 Foss, Alvira L.
360 Foss, George.
361 Foss, Deborah G.
363 Foss, Martin H.
362 Foss, Lizzie H.
410 Foss, George B.
25 Fox, Isaac.
33 Fox, Isaac, 2d,

317 Gale, Hannah P.
272 George, Moses.
273 George, Sarah D.
207 George, Hannah H.
199 George, Abigail C.
79 Giddings, Jacob.
198 Giddings, Elizabeth P.
158 Giddings, Mary.
171 Glines, Jonathan.
172 Glines, Eliza N.
306 Goss, Annette B.
216 Graham, Jane.
325 Greenough, William J.

332 Hadley, Louise C.	217 Merrill, Adeline M.	307 Smith, Gilman R.
333 Hadley, Louise J.	131 Mills, Sarah L.	308 Smith, Adaline H.
69 Hale, Lydia.	388 Mitchell, Pamelia H.	28 Southmayd, Ruth B.
132 Hale, Jonathan L.	61 Moody, Rebecca B.	38 Spencer, Statira.
135 Hale, Fanny H.	194 Moody, Sarah G.	108 Spencer, Israel.
24 Hall, Abigail B.	96 Morrison, Robert.	109 Spencer, Molly T.
17 Hart, Huldab B.	103 Morrison, Anna F.	155 Spencer, Arvilla C.
241 Harwood, Louise C.	159 Morrison, Ebenezer B.	262 Spencer, Hannah B.
253 Hatch, Catherine C.	128 Morrison, Eliza B.	265 Spencer, George.
183 Hayes. John P.	282 Morse, Mehitabel H.	266 Spencer, Sarah B.
366 Hill, Samuel C.	385 Moses, Isaac S.	274 Spencer, Jane C.
367 Hill, Eliza L.	386 Moses, Margaret M.	319 Stanton, Martha B.
346 Hodgdon, Ezekiel H.	400 Moulton, Bessie E.	349 Stickney, Benjamin.
347 Hodgdon, Almira D.		264 Stickney, Phebe P.
404 Hodgdon, Harriet A.	60 Noyes, Joanna B.	350 Stickney, Hermon C.
280 Hodge, John M.	71 Noyes, Sarah.	351 Stickney, Mary E.
291 Hodge, William A.	256 Noyes, Harriet L.	392 Stickney, William H.
168 Holmes, Caroline C.		393 Stickney, Edwin H.
195 Holmes, Susanna K.	95 Orr, Sarah B.	398 Stickney, Charles O.
409 Holmes, Norris.	383 Osgood, Clara.	402 Stickney, Laura A.
208 Homan, Harriet W.		222 Stone, Apphia F.
359 Homan, Jane B.	177 Page, Lucy C.	
104 Houston, Esther W.	178 Page, Abigail C.	47 Taylor, Mary W.
206 Houston, Lydia.	243 Page, Caroline M.	157 Taylor, Sally C.
279 Howe, Elizabeth C.	37 Palmer, Martha T.	407 Taylor, Gilman R.
269 Howell, Alvira H.	39 Palmer, Elizabeth.	188 Taylor, Polly B.
336 Huntress, Martha B.	130 Palmer, Eleanor M.	298 Taylor, Mary W.
229 Huse, Daniel M.	145 Palmer, Rebecca P.	374 Thornton, S. Frances.
230 Huse, Eliza D.	316 Palmer, Jane B.	395 Thornton, Horatio H.
	167 Percival, Harriet.	205 Thurston, Martha M.
191 Jackson, Sally C.	251 Pillsbury, Daniel.	380 Tirrell, M. Carrie.
92 Johnson, William.	259 Pillsbury, Betsey B.	1 Tupper, Nathaniel.
136 Johnson, Hervey.	210 Pray, Caroline M.	2 Tupper, Hannah F.
137 Johnson, Sarah D.	335 Pronk, Sarah P.	
164 Johnson, Mary L.	263 Pulsifer, Joseph.	391 Wallace, William.
187 Johnson, Alice M.	36 Pulsifer, Abigail W.	303 Wallace, Hannah B.
283 Johnson, Susan H.	112 Pulsifer, Daniel.	406 Wallace, George W.
401 Johnson, Hester E.	202 Pulsifer, Betsey S.	364 Webber, Emily B.
377 Joslyn, Charles C.	113 Pulsifer, John.	384 Webber, Emily E.
	179 Pulsifer, Polly P.	97 Whitney, Otis.
175 Keniston, Mary B.	277 Pulsifer, Martha L.	34 Whitney, Sarah T.
353 Kennedy, Rubamah A.	184 Pulsifer, Caroline.	326 Whitney, Mary F.
375 Kennedy, Amanda S.	221 Pulsifer, Abigail.	7 Willey, Deborah.
118 Kimball, John W.	258 Pulsifer, Joseph, Jr.	15 Willey, Darius.
281 Kimball, Abigail D.	261 Pulsifer, Elizabeth.	19 Willey, Mary W.
	295 Pulsifer, Moses.	41 Willey, Abel.
117 Ladd, James,	296 Pulsifer, David B.	50 Willey, Miriam.
102 Ladd, Charity W.	330 Pulsifer, Isabella W.	56 Willey, Diadate.
106 Ladd, Mary B.	343 Pulsifer, Thomas S.	57 Willey, Mary B.
223 Ladd, Thankful O.	342 Pulsifer, Hannah P.	67 Willey, Isaac, Jr.
309 Leuce, Calvin.	365 Pulsifer, Charles W.	68 Willey, Leonard.
231 Leuce, Sally M.	318 Pulsifer, Malvina C.	83 Willey, Lydia S.
76 Little, Lydia B.	371 Pulsifer, Sarah L.	100 Willey, Darius, Jr.
78 Little, Ebenezer, Jr.		101 Willey, Mary P.
133 Little, Phebe P.	299 Reed, Mary E.	138 Willey, Susan R.
150 Little, James.	192 Robertson, Hall.	173 Willey, Austin.
151 Little, Polly C.	193 Robertson, Eliza K.	189 Willey, Judith R.
235 Little, Mary.	11 Rogers, Joshua.	182 Willey, Worcester.
242 Little, Charles.	26 Rogers, Sarah N.	213 Willey, Selden C.
252 Little, Sarah C.	72 Rogers, William.	275 Willey, Elizabeth D.
373 Little, Clarissa B.	271 Rogers, Elizabeth G.	297 Willey, M. Melvina.
382 Little, Frances L.	74 Rogers, John.	214 Willey, Emeline.
369 Litchfield, Frances J.	75 Rogers, Abigail B.	237 Willey, Samuel H.
	80 Rogers, Leonard.	338 Willey, Charles H.
247 Marden. Mark.		399 Willey, Esther E.
62 Marsh, Edmund.	190 Sanborn, Emeline.	45 Woodbury, Hannah T.
44 Marsh, Eunice C.	218 Sanborn, Sally P.	110 Woodbury, Margaret B.
51 Marsh, Thomas.	267 Sanborn, Hazen.	220 Woodbury, Lucy.
52 Marsh, Eliza W.	268 Sanborn, Ann M.	54 Woodman, Judith M.
53 Marsh, Christopher.	285 Sanborn, Jesse A.	27 Wooster, David.
63 Marsh, Washington.	286 Sanborn, Sarah S.	81 Wooster, John.
64 Marsh, Rhoda W.	337 Sanborn, Sarah E.	10 Wyatt, Daniel.
232 Marsh, Newton.	294 Sargent, Elizabeth C.	43 Wyatt, Abigail A.
233 Marsh, Lydia H.	276 Shedd, Eliza R.	226 Wyatt, George W.
356 Marsh, Julia Ann.	248 Shedd, Henry E.	203 Wyatt, Martha P.
143 Merrill, James.	289 Shedd, Caroline L.	301 Wyatt, Henry D.
144 Merrill, Sarah F.	304 Shedd, M Elizabeth.	314 Wyatt, Daniel.
260 Merrill, Gardner.	278 Skinner, Caroline E.	

www.ingramcontent.com/pod-product-compliance
Lightning Source LLC
Chambersburg PA
CBHW020333090426
42735CB00009B/1515